THE PARENTING TODDLERS WORKBOOK

THE PARENTING TODDLERS WORKBOOK

MANAGE YOUR CHILD'S MOODS, POTENTIAL, AND WELL-BEING

KATIE PENRY, PsyD

Illustrations by
PENELOPE DULLAGHAN

ROCKRIDGE
PRESS

For general information on our other products and services or to obtain technical support, please contact our Customer Care Department within the United States at (866) 744-2665, or outside the United States at (510) 253-0500.

Rockridge Press publishes its books in a variety of electronic and print formats. Some content that appears in print may not be available in electronic books, and vice versa.

Interior and Cover Designer: Angela Navarra
Art Producer: Sara Feinstein
Editor: Mo Mozuch
Production Editor: Matt Burnett

Illustrations © 2020 Penelope Dullaghan.
Illustrator photograph courtesy of © Michelle Craig Photography.
Author photograph courtesy of © Laura Rowe Photography.

ISBN: Print 978-1-64611-849-6 | eBook 978-1-64611-850-2

R0

For my children.

CONTENTS

INTRODUCTION

Setting the tone for a parenting workbook is challenging. I am a parent with two small children, ages four and six. And like many parents, I have suffered the misplaced advice of Grocery Store Gail, every town's friendly expert stranger. Her disapproving stare cast a harsh spotlight in which my children occasionally eat refined sugar and curse at the cat.

Parenting puts us in a vulnerable position. Many of our choices are on full public display in parks and schools and while shopping. And like everyone around us, we know that the stakes are high. *Children really are our future*, and society puts pressure on parents to do their job well—for the sake of the whole tribe. Giving advice is a deeply human instinct that serves a valuable purpose. The problem, of course, is *judgment*.

Unfair and unnecessary judgment can consume parenthood. According to Zero to Three's 2015 *National Parent Survey,* 9 out of 10 parents across all economic, gender, and racial segments say that they feel unfairly judged. "Strangers in the community" top the list of perpetrators, followed closely by (drumroll, please) . . . "in-laws." Nine out of 10 is a startling number. It means that 90 percent of my readers are coming to this book with a measure of pain, **hoping that I won't be yet another stranger who listens poorly, judges unfairly, and leaves a trail of shaming commentary in my wake**.

To help overcome this fear, I want to lay out some of my core beliefs right here, right up front. You can read the few short paragraphs that follow and decide for yourself whether I might be a trusted companion:

Parents are the most powerful agents of change in the world. Americans are obsessed with superheroes, as evidenced by the billions of dollars we pour (annually) into comic book movie franchises. But listen, who needs superpowers when you can love a child well? Learn to do *that*, and it's you who will save the world.

Your child is resilient. You can always, always, *always* improve the well-being of any child, without exception. Your challenges and failures might loom large, but there is nothing more powerful than the love, understanding, curiosity, and acceptance of a parent. Nothing. Children and their parents can heal. Sometimes it just takes a little work.

Perfection isn't the goal. Brief periods of disorganization in the parent–toddler relationship are expected and normal. Be it anger, the collapse of empathy and kindness, or impatience—it's okay. Parental failures and their repair are an invaluable part of child development. We are shooting for "good enough," not perfect.

Parents deserve accurate information. Oh, man. So many lovely parents have walked through my office door saddled with guilt and fear from the misinformation available in the mommy blogosphere. You deserve better. I know how to acquire, read, and interpret research statistics—the kind of research you get from universities, not gossip and anecdotes from the local PTA. If I say, "Research says," I mean, "a reputable source of peer-reviewed science has indicated . . ." Occasionally, you'll see titles and dates noted in parentheses. These are actual citations to actual research that you can actually read yourself, if you so choose.

In the first part of this book, you will find a review of toddler-parenting basics. We will cover tantrums, growth patterns, play ideas, eating complications, and everything in between. In part 2, you'll have opportunities to complete exercises that will deepen your understanding and strengthen your relationships with your children. In both parts, I will be trying to speak to you with the same empathic and gentle guidance that you will be learning to implement in your own home.

I will be passionate about your power and ability, I won't judge your imperfections, and I will be giving you dependable information. I hope you feel as though you can trust me because good things are in store.

HOW TO USE THIS WORKBOOK

This workbook is not homework. Try to view the various worksheets as *opportunities*, rather than exercises, to deepen your understanding and strengthen your relation-ship with your child. You will find opportunities to articulate your family's values. You will develop parenting strategies that keep these values in mind. You will have opportunities to become increasingly intentional about your discipline, praise, and interventions.

If your time is very limited and your needs are immediate, you can use this workbook to troubleshoot. The headings and subheadings should be obvious enough to make navigation quick and easy. If you are new to parenting or are hoping for more trans-formative action, you can move through the book a little at the time, slowly, from start to finish. The opportunities within these pages can be private or shared. Use them to create conversation and diminish disagreement with your co-parent or your child's caregiver. Or create a parenting group of your own and share the exercises together.

My hope is that you'll have everything you need to gain greater insight into your child's development and that the exercises, once completed, will continue to be a source of wisdom and reflection.

PART ONE

TODDLERS
ARE MORE THAN
TANTRUMS

According to the dictionary definition, "to toddle" means "to move with short, unsteady steps." It can be implied, then, that a "toddler" is simply a child who "toddles." This definition is easy enough yet woefully inadequate (and mildly comical). For many of today's parents, describing the toddler years according to the child's unsteady gait is akin to calling Godzilla "a clumsy lizard." We get that Godzilla is a reptile, *but that hardly seems to be the issue.*

Like Godzilla, toddlers have a reputation for destruction, bad temper, and terror-filled walks through the city. Toddlers can scream, cry, make pernicious demands, and breathe fire with the same zeal as an irritated and over-radiated monster. They also have the most extraordinary capacity for growth, connection, development, and learning. In her *New York Times* bestselling book *The Conscious Parent*, Dr. Shefali Tsabary makes the case that interacting with toddlers can even be a path to spiritual awakening and enlightenment (insert wide-eyed emoji here).

The first three years of a child's life are so crucial that several massively funded initiatives have been launched to support parents as they navigate this powerful period of growth. See, for example, the National Scientific Council on the Developing Child, Harvard's Center on the Developing Child, Zero to Three, The Center for the Study of Social Policy, Sesame Workshop, and so on. The common conviction is that *stronger families lead to stronger foundations, and stronger foundations lead to the kind of outcomes that even governments can't afford to ignore* (Center for the Developing Child at Harvard University, 2010).

In the first part of this book, we will discuss the key components of healthy and happy toddler parenting. I will consolidate all the wonderful research (that you don't have time to read) into short snippets that are digestible and easy to apply. The components discussed in this first part of the workbook will be revisited throughout the exercises as we find new opportunities at each age to become more intentional. The goals are to strengthen your child and to deepen your relationship through understanding and purposeful application.

HOW TODDLERS GROW

When we understand how the child's brain grows, it becomes much easier to be an effective and caring parent. A great place to start is the age-old "nature versus nurture" debate. Is your child more heavily influenced by their genetic makeup or their environment? Recently, researchers have shown that "nature *together with* nurture" is a better way of considering the topic. The language of "versus" is no longer helpful or accurate. Genes turn on and off, express themselves or remain dormant, all according to early experiences and repeated use. In other words, your "nurture" deeply affects their "nature."

With each new publication it becomes clearer that early relationships are the fuel that drive development forward. The experiences children have during these early years actually shape the architecture of the brain and the development of motor skills. By understanding how your toddler grows, we can now proclaim with confidence that you—not fancy toys or expensive early learning experiences–are your child's great compatriot, comrade, and co-worker. Your child's brain has one great asset and encourager: YOU!

Brain development continues throughout life, but we now estimate that nearly one million new neural connections are formed every second in the first few years of life (Center on the Developing Child at Harvard University, 2015). Plus, when parents are warmly attuned and responsive during this time of rapid growth, absolutely incredible things happen to these new connections. During the early years, you and your child's brain work together to lay the foundation for all future development. This includes the critical skills of success, resilience, and lifelong learning.

Over time, this proliferation of new neural pathways slows, unused connections are lost or "pruned," and new neural pathways form at a slower pace. But those connections that are made and reinforced early in life provide either a weak or strong foundation for the connections that will form later.

We can't be certain about the exact age at which this proliferation slows; the process of brain growth is just too relational and dynamic. But parents can ensure that neural connections are being made in a way that facilitates healthy maturation and intelligence. They do this by staying warmly attuned and responsive during the toddler years. When children feel safe, known, and understood, the foundation for all growth—including emotional management, communication, and problem solving—is made sturdier and more reliable.

As you were taught in high school biology, genes (*nature*) are in fact the blueprint for the formation of neural circuits and pathways. But now we know that relational interactions (*nurture*) determine which of these circuits will be activated and reinforced or muted and turned off. This could sound threatening, but don't be scared. It is true that you are very important, but the things that are important about you aren't your material resources, marital status, education, or even previous experience. The things that truly matter for your child's growth are simple and achievable: your careful attention, your thoughtful reaction, and your appropriate responses.

THE DANGERS OF SCREEN TIME

Your careful attention, your thoughtful reaction, and your appropriate responses are the things that matter most when it comes to the healthy development of your toddler. Isn't that good to know? But there is a problem, and I am going to be as honest as possible about it. Research continues to unequivocally indicate that the overuse of screens *by parents* interrupts all (yes, ALL) of these things (Radesky, Miller, Rosenblum, Appugliese, Kaciroti, and Lumeng, 2015).

I bet you thought this section was going to strictly address your child's screen time. Nope. Caregiver screen use matters, too.

The absolute imperative building block for all mental health, learning, and well-being (and without which a child is critically injured) is *your attuned and appropriately responsive interactions with your child*. Your child cannot grow, cannot learn about the self, cannot learn about relationships, cannot learn about the world, and cannot create imperative neurological structures for learning without your attention, your eyeballs, and your face. Your gaze is *foundational* for your toddler's well-being. When parents become frequently, immersively distracted, they begin to deprive their children of eye contact, a shared and appreciative gaze, a focused audience, and an appropriately responsive play partner. These things are critical for healthy development.

Screens (e-readers, tablets, phones, and televisions) are endlessly accessible, so it's tempting to use them as a means of distraction. Their convenience is undeniable. Feeling like you are the constant source of entertainment and instruction for your child can be exhausting. But here is the catch: Population-based studies continue to show that excessive screen use in early childhood is associated with *even more exhausting* problems later (Reid Chassiakos, 2016). These future problems are big. They include stuff like delays in attention, thinking, language, and social skills; poor health and childhood obesity; poor sleep quality; and behavior issues like aggression, acting out, and tantrums.

Parents think that they love the convenience of screens until they come to me with a kindergartener who is unable to self-regulate, manage attention, initiate activity, or transition between tasks. These are things that we know develop in the context of responsive relationships with caregivers. This means that *all parents and their children* need to be using screens less. Toddlers grow in relationships, and screens interrupt relationships. According to the *American Academy of Pediatrics*, children younger than two years should almost never be given screen time. If a screen of some kind is offered, it should be done together with the parent. Children ages two to five years should be given no more than one hour a day of screen time.

MILESTONES

Children grow taller and stronger. They also develop skills and neural connections. Typically, the word *milestones* refers to developmental acquisitions and not to physical growth. Physical growth is just too idiosyncratic to be monitored in the context of a mass-produced book like this one. Child development, however, follows a trajectory that does make "milestones" a useful concept. These helpful milestones are consistently categorized along four different axes of development:

Muscles—Muscle development is tracked along the lines of three major motor groups. These are *gross motor* (large muscle groups, like the kind used to accomplish walking and crawling), *fine motor* (small muscle groups, like fingers), and *oral motor* (the muscles used to maneuver the mouth).

Language—Language development is also subdivided into three skill sets. Parents tend to think only about *expressive language skills*—that is, speaking words and expressing needs—but *receptive language skills* are equally valuable and fun to notice. Children can understand what you're saying (and follow directions) long before they can respond with their own words. *Nonverbal communication skills* are usually the first form of expression and can become quite sophisticated. These include pointing and grunting as well as other sounds, gestures, and facial expressions.

Social and emotional—I am regularly baffled by how many parents completely ignore this element of their child's development. And yet these milestones are equally (if not more) important for lifelong success and learning. These milestones are learned in relationships and are stunted when relationships are unattuned, absent, or inadequate. They include things like engaging others, making friends, making eye contact, and having self-esteem and personal agency. These tend to be my largest concern and the focus of my work.

Intelligence—You might have heard this referred to as "cognitive development." Children are constantly having to take in information and make sense of it. These milestones typically refer to the child's ability to problem-solve, think spatially and creatively, and determine cause and effect.

At the start of each section in part 2 of this book, I will provide a brief description of the typical capacities and achievements of children at a specific age (12 months, 18 months, 2 years, and so forth). The information will be structured so that you can ignore the age, if you prefer, and focus on the milestones to find the most relevant approaches. For instance, if your child is three years old but seems to still be working hard on the developmental achievements of a typical two-year-old, then use the intervention strategies and approaches in the chapter about two-year-olds to create a benevolent and gracious environment. When it comes to discipline and training, it is best for parents to accommodate the particular needs of their child. Meet them where they are, not where you think they should be.

DON'T GET MIRED IN MILESTONES

The idea of milestones can trigger a flood of insecurities about a child's delays and their many causes. In my experience, however, parents of toddlers are more comforted by a gentle presentation of milestones than parents of infants seem to be. This is because toddlers' milestones are more dynamic and flexible. They are also heavily influenced by relationships and interactions with parents. A new skill can be encouraged to blossom with only a little guidance. If you are very worried about your child's delays, though, speak to your pediatrician as soon as possible. Early intervention programs among toddlers are important and powerful.

In general, though, it is good to hold milestones with a loose grip. A tight, competitive approach is almost never helpful. It might help to remember that typical development has a surprisingly wide range. For instance, the "normal" age for standing is between 7 months and 17 months and can be affected by a huge number of circumstances.

I like to discuss milestones and typical behaviors because many parents are comforted to know, for instance, that biting is normal at certain ages and stages. I like to use milestones to reassure parents that "it's okay if your child is doing behavior X." This less evaluative and academic approach to milestones helps parents be more accepting and strategic about their discipline. It also reduces anxiety. For instance, a two-year-old's normal hitting behavior can be purposefully and graciously addressed without the shame and overreaction parents display when they fear their child is becoming a psychopathic deviant. Two-year-olds occasionally hit and bite. Is that behavior okay? No. But do you need to be worried about a future prison sentence? Absolutely not.

THE FOUR PARTS OF HEALTHY PARENTING

For the sake of keeping this book simple and easy to use, we can group most of the parents' major functions into one of four categories: *wellness, learning, boundaries and routines, and discipline*. I feel that these four categories are excellent umbrella terms for just about everything we do to meet the toddler's core needs. Some of us are masters of wellness but struggle with setting boundaries and maintaining routines. Others desperately struggle with discipline but can teach their child a new language in five days. No parent is bad in all areas, and no parent is instinctively strong in all areas. You definitely have strengths to lean into as you learn.

Over the next few pages I will familiarize you with these four concepts and the toddler-centric activities that fall into each category. Keep in mind the areas in which you feel confident and strong and where you feel like you might need extra support. The activities in part 2 are divided according to these categories. I hope this will help you easily navigate the book as you seek to round out your skill set and become a robust, effective parent with a ton of valuable skills.

WELLNESS

Keeping your child physically and emotionally healthy is the flagship goal of this workbook. In the wellness sections of part 2, we will focus on the core competencies that will create and sustain lifelong health and well-being for your child. These competencies include play, nutrition, and sleep. It also includes emotional competencies like temperament recognition, collaboration among caregivers, and the parent's mental health. The wellness section works hard to address the core needs of your child at each stage and age.

Toddlers are *very* responsive to the physical needs of their body. They are also very responsive to less obvious needs like repetition, routine, and the experience of feeling seen. Keep reading the following sections to ensure that you are giving your child every opportunity to thrive, throw fewer tantrums, and live their best life. Follow through with learning your child's core needs by completing each wellness section in part 2.

Let's Eat!

Toddlers still need good nutrition to help their bodies continue to develop optimally, and their palates expand as the kind of foods they can eat grows and changes. Also, they will begin to learn about eating well and taking care of themselves. The toddler years are a great time to help your child begin their journey toward lifelong health and avoid the pitfalls of childhood obesity. They can begin to learn about the food groups and the reasons certain items keep appearing on their plate (for example, vegetables). Introducing my toddlers to new foods was one of my favorite stages. Mealtime doesn't have to be miserable.

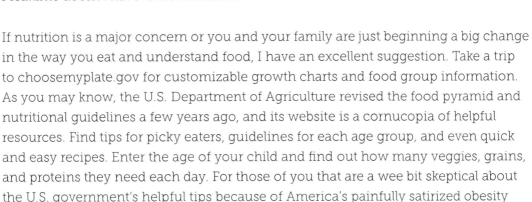

If nutrition is a major concern or you and your family are just beginning a big change in the way you eat and understand food, I have an excellent suggestion. Take a trip to choosemyplate.gov for customizable growth charts and food group information. As you may know, the U.S. Department of Agriculture revised the food pyramid and nutritional guidelines a few years ago, and its website is a cornucopia of helpful resources. Find tips for picky eaters, guidelines for each age group, and even quick and easy recipes. Enter the age of your child and find out how many veggies, grains, and proteins they need each day. For those of you that are a wee bit skeptical about the U.S. government's helpful tips because of America's painfully satirized obesity epidemic, I get it. But I can assure you that the problem isn't with our scientists. The U.S. Department of Agriculture has done some excellent work to equip choosemyplate.gov with terrific tools to teach healthy habits and shape health-conscious children.

Play Time!

I cannot emphasize enough the importance of play. Although all parents seem to implicitly know that food is important, the importance of play is more easily overlooked. And yet it is fundamental. Fred Rogers, of the revolutionary show *Mister Rogers' Neighborhood,* once said, "Play is the work of childhood. Play is a very serious thing indeed. Play gives children a chance to practice what they are learning . . . ."

In each section, I will offer tips for playing with children at different ages. But I think the first step in playing well is simply appreciating the important work that happens when a child plays. For many parents, simply knowing that what seems silly, redundant, or pointless is actually valuable can help them engage with their child's play.

Play is crucial in the child's acquisition of reality. Transitioning from the necessary narcissistic delusion of infancy (this whole world revolves around me) to the reality of life (I am just one member of a community) is pretty difficult. Play is the space where children learn to accept boundaries and rules.

Play helps toddlers take different perspectives and learn empathy. For instance, when Mom says, "No," the child can then play at being mom and draw closer to understanding a world (reality) in which her rules and conduct might be necessary.

Play helps children transition into new environments and life stages.
When you introduce useful tools for play like books, blocks, puppets, arts, and music, you are essentially giving a child more tools to be successful in this transition from play to reality.

Play is where children acquire new skills. A lot of motor skill development happens in the context of play. Other relationship skills, like listening, cooperation, and sharing, are also acquired in play.

Play can be a dramatic platform to experiment with big, scary emotions. Toddlerhood isn't all cake and crackers. Life is happening, and sometimes life events can be troubling. Play is the context in which children can make sense of hardship and of events they find difficult to understand.

Bath Time!

It is never too early to teach kids some basic hygiene. They need to learn to wash their hands, brush their teeth, and care for their bodies. Plus, the bath time routine can be very grounding for the child. It's intimate time with the parent that can ease the transition into the mystery and separation of night. That one-on-one time is so special, and those clean feet and hands are important.

Nap Time!

Like play, nap time is incredibly important. Parents suffer and struggle with grumpy children, terrible tempers, and dinnertime meltdowns more often than they should because of one simple (fixable) problem: fatigue. All that rapid brain growth and skill acquisition is absolutely exhausting. If your child doesn't sleep well and doesn't at the very least have quiet time during the day, you're setting yourself (and them) up for failure during the afternoon. You're also limiting how much you can do that evening. When children don't nap, you have to be very careful about afternoon outings or fun activities because you don't want them to suffer with tantrums or overstimulation.

The approach to nap time should always be one of utmost respect: Your children listen, and they are learning. They are good kids who want to do well. When they are too tired, they can't meet their goals or learn new skills. However difficult, the enforcement of naps prevents more suffering than it causes. The research is pretty clear—fatigue is real, and naps are an invaluable asset in the growth and behavioral management of children. Give your children the opportunity to succeed. Help them nap. I'll cover some tips and help you plan for nap time in part 2.

LEARNING

In a world where sophisticated flashcards, apps, and toys are pushed on us daily, many parents are shocked to learn that *they* (and not the fancy classes or toys they provide) are the most important tool for their toddler's learning, cognitive growth, and school readiness. It is the quality of a baby's early relationships and the type of loving experiences you provide that make the biggest impact on their learning. For toddlers, the type of learning many parents emphasize (and rightfully so) is school readiness. We want our children to begin school with gusto, prepared for a confidence-inducing experience that will set the stage for lifelong learning.

In order to be school ready, however, the emphasis truly is less on letters, numbers, shapes, and colors than on language, literacy, thinking, and social-emotional skills. Toddlers need to develop a strong foundation in their thinking and communication skills. They need to be able to exert self-control, initiate activities, sustain their attention, and have self-confidence. The great news about helping toddlers learn these skills is that formal "teaching" activities aren't required. All that is necessary is your consistent, loving, and attuned everyday interactions. Throughout part 2, I will provide information so that you can be particularly responsive to your child's needs at different ages. But as a whole, the emphasis should be built on gentle and responsive guidance that pays attention to the child's curiosities and abilities.

In each section of part 2, I'll include more direct ways to facilitate the core competencies of learning at each age. But, for now, you can begin to familiarize yourself with the basic elements of learning during the toddler years.

Language and Literacy

Learning to read and write starts well before kindergarten. You can develop language and literacy skills through everyday loving interactions. In fact, this is the best way to get started. You and your child should be reading together, singing songs, telling stories, and talking all the time. Your child can understand way more than they can say, so share your observations and experiences as often as possible. When your child makes attempts at new words and sounds, engage and encourage them.

Thinking

During the toddler years, your child's ability to think about increasingly complex problems and solutions is astounding. You can and should encourage early math and science skills by embracing everyday "teachable moments." Use your daily interactions to notice patterns, shapes, and colors. You can count together as you climb stairs, pass red cars, or begin noticing fingers and toes. Introduce new materials, novel situations, and creativity during pretend play and imaginative exercises. As improbable as it may seem, even the foundations for science, technology, engineering, and math competencies are best built in the context of simple, relational exchanges.

Social-Emotional Competence

In the past, there has been a heavy emphasis on building toddler academic skills to ensure school readiness. But an overwhelming body of research is now demonstrating that school success is heavily influenced by a child's social and emotional competencies. One of the biggest standout skills in this category is, of course, self-control. But there are a lot of dimensions to social and emotional learning. It includes stuff like self-esteem and confidence, personal agency (planning and carrying out actions), patience, persistence, conflict resolution, empathy, and communication skills. The catch is that we also now know that these things don't develop on their own. They develop in the context of caring relationships.

WANT YOUR TODDLER TO LEARN? USE SERVE AND RETURN

Let's get down to brass tacks. Scientifically speaking, there is nothing new about the importance of the child's relationships. Relationships matter, and we know it. The thing that is shaking the social and neurological sciences to their core is *just how foundational relationships are to every area of development*. Responsive and caring relationships are critical to optimal brain development, social development, and *all* elements of learning. Saying relationships matter to toddlers is like saying water matters to fish. It is the scale of importance and the breadth of impact that have come into breathtaking focus.

To clarify the important elements of responsive relationships, Harvard's Center on the Developing Child has created valuable instructions for the basics of effective parent-child interaction. They call this subset of responsivity *serve and return*. One of the most impactful parts of a relationship—the part that we think does a lot of the heavy lifting when it comes to brain-building—is back-and-forth interactions. The serve and return literature takes the most transformative element of relationships and breaks it into five teachable steps. I adore Harvard's work here because the researchers have completely divested themselves of any academic haughtiness (it happens) and acknowledged that the basics matter. It is very hard to articulate basic relationship dynamics, but they have done it beautifully and simply.

STEP ONE: Notice the serve and share the child's focus of attention.

A "serve" is a verbal or nonverbal attention-seeking gesture such as calling out for you to see something, looking and pointing, or making a facial expression. Look for opportunities to notice what your child is noticing.

Why? This encourages the toddler to explore while reinforcing your bond.

STEP TWO: Return the serve by supporting and encouraging.

The "return" is some kind of confirmation that you notice the same thing. You can make a facial expression or say, "Yes! I see." You can pick up the thing the child is pointing to and hand it to them.

Why? This helps the child feel known and understood while rewarding their curiosity.

STEP THREE: Give it a name.

Try to connect language to your child's experience by labeling or naming what the toddler is seeing, doing, or feeling. If the kid angrily points to the crayon on the ground say, "You're making an angry face and pointing at that crayon." Then put the crayon back on the table.

Why? This builds the language part of the brain. It also helps the child make sense of the world around them.

STEP FOUR: Take turns and wait.

Every time you return a child's serve, stay engaged and attentive long enough for them to respond. Waiting is crucial. They need the time, and your attention encourages the interaction to keep going.

Why? This helps kids learn self-control. It also helps them understand social interaction and relationships.

STEP FIVE: Practice endings and beginnings.

Children signal when they are ready to move on or be finished with an activity. You can practice ending an activity and beginning a new activity by participating in serve and return until they are finished.

Why? This encourages children to take the lead in safe, structured interactions. It also makes more brain-building serve and return interactions possible.

BOUNDARIES AND ROUTINES

There are few things more important than *responsive relationships* in the life and learning trajectory of your toddler. The major exception is *safety*. This is because children can hardly acquire new knowledge or skills unless they feel safe. When a child feels unsafe, learning and development (and sometimes even growth) are stunted. When children feel chronically unsafe, it becomes toxic to the brain's architecture.

The fantastic thing about safety is that we can significantly enhance a child's sense of security, even in very difficult circumstances, through the use of consistent rules, limits, and routines. This may surprise you. Adults don't respond to limits in the same way that children do. Routine can be comforting to us, but it doesn't necessarily make adults feel secure. Toddlers are very different. For them, boundaries, routines, and repetition are the brain food of childhood because they create feelings of safety.

No matter how you might personally enjoy (or not) a life of predictability, children thrive on it. They are uniquely created to flourish within a consistent relationship with reliable expectations. Consistent limit-setting and reliable expectations are one of your child's fundamental needs. Knowing the hopes you have for your child, what values your family appreciates, and what kind of character you want your toddler to have can help you think intentionally about what kind of boundaries and expectations you want to create and enforce. In part 2, I will offer you several opportunities to consider these things and create a more intentional and purposeful plan for developing and enforcing reasonable boundaries for your child.

The other part of this safety puzzle is *routines*. In the next few short paragraphs, I will walk you through different ideas for helpful routines as well as ways to maintain your routines despite complicated schedules. The goal isn't to create exact schedules and perfectly identical days. Schedule and routine are different.

What Is a Routine?

Routines are predictable activities that happen every day of the week, sometimes more than once each day. *Schedules* are associated with the clock. You can be late on a schedule. You can never be late for a routine. That said, when children recognize that events are occurring at roughly the same time and in the same way each day, they develop memory and organization skills. When routines occur on a relatively predictable schedule, children feel less anxious.

There are many ways that routines can be implemented to buttress and secure your child's development without causing boredom and strain. Rote perfection and identical days aren't the goal. Occasionally events like doctor's appointments, changes in the parent's schedule, or changes in the caregiver can disrupt a toddler's routines. When this happens, we simply accept with love that the child will be more combustible. They may show their confusion and upset feelings in big ways. We can help by being understanding and explaining changes as or before they happen.

We create empathy, connection, and comfort when we understand that children grow very attached to routines and are disrupted when things change. There is no shame in disruption, but it is hard on the toddler, and we should provide kind, empathic support.

Bedtime

For most of my children's lives, bedtime has been our most treasured routine. Besides changing clothes and diapers, it is probably the first routine parents establish. For us, little has changed. My kids bathe themselves now, but the pattern of events—bath, jammies, teeth, book, songs, sleep—has stayed the same. For most healthy families, sleep represents the first and most significant separation. Even though it is temporary and necessary, drifting off into sleep is still a drifting away from mom and dad. Sleep and dreams are mysterious—and the room is dark—so a peaceful routine is paramount. Creating a bedtime routine that provides hygiene, touch, and a moment to reflect with gratitude on the day's events has been shown to be very powerful. We also take the opportunity to read with our children every single night. Incorporating reading into a treasured routine is smart because it communicates the priority that reading together should have in the life of the family. It also provides a bit of accountability. When you make reading a part of the routine (rather than a random act of entertainment), your children will insist that you do it every night. Reading outside a routine is also awesome, but put it square in the middle of a child's valued rhythm, and they will never let you forget it.

NIGHTMARES AND NIGHT TERRORS

Nightmares begin at about three years of age and typically happen in the second half of the night. They occur during REM sleep, and the child usually remembers them. Nightmares shouldn't be occurring every single night. If the toddler is coming to your room nightly, using the excuse of a nightmare to garner extra cuddles from you, that is a separate behavior that needs to be addressed. Nightmares that actually occur with frequency need to be discussed during the day. What is happening or has happened in their routine to cause such sadness and darkness during their dream cycle?

Night terrors on the other hand tend to happen in the first half of the evening. They can be startling to the kids, but to the parents they are terrifying. The children may or may not remember waking up in a total, inconsolable panic. The parent, though, rarely forgets. Night terrors usually occur at about the same time each night. The best way to stop them is to set an alarm for a few minutes before they typically occur. This brief waking is usually enough to stem the tide. It is also wise to address the child's level of fatigue and perhaps get them to bed earlier. Frequent night terrors are a sign of overtiredness in toddlers.

Rules and Chores

Successfully following rules and completing chores are estimable acts that build confidence, especially when you acknowledge with pride the help your toddler is offering or the way they are choosing to respect you. It is never too early to slowly introduce rules and ways they can help you. These helpful moments are a fantastic way to comingle routine with boundaries and expectations. Toddlers can pick up books, close the refrigerator, stir the muffin mix, and shelve their toys. They might sometimes be clumsy and uncoordinated, but offering these moments to accomplish helpful actions is important. Too often, parents allow the incredibly important narcissism that naturally occurs during infancy to continue a hair too long, even into the toddler years. When expectations and the rules of communal living are then introduced later, it is confusing to the child. They are then more likely to resist chores and rules. It is better to have the habits of helping built into your routines in simple ways as soon as your toddler is capable of them. It is always smart to approach your child with respect. This includes showing them gratitude for the help they can contribute and the important role they play in the family.

Potty Training

Potty training is an intimate affair that is best done in a very responsive manner. Determining when children are ready should be individualized. It is typically earlier for girls than boys, but again, listen to the needs of your child. As the child begins to potty train, some important routines will begin to surface. For the sake of their success in the effort, respect these routines and you'll reduce resistance. You may want to encourage use of the potty before leaving the house and when getting home. Also make a trip to the potty when you first arrive somewhere and every night right before bed. Folding difficult moments into a treasured routine can be a powerful way to increase compliance and success. A lot of parents have success by using the three-day jump-start method and then creating very consistent routines in the days or weeks that follow. I learned all about the three-day method on YouTube and still hold that this is the best way to potty train. The three-day method is an approach to potty training in which the child's next phase of toileting is kick-started with an intensive three days of pantsless wandering and playing in the house, peppered with frequent trips to the potty. It is fun for the kid and intense for the parent but has the potential to make for a really lovely and intimate weekend with children and their parent(s).

Getting Dressed

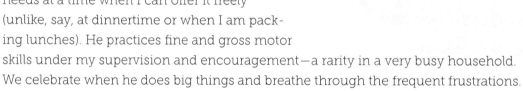

Is there a sweeter moment in my day than when my toddler and I sit on the floor together and get him dressed? Maybe. But this is certainly a treasured time. He can be wiggly and mischievous, but we both love this ritual. It is a moment for us to mindfully reconnect to each other. He will often hold my face, give me kisses, and tell me he loves me. I return the favor. We breathe and wrestle and laugh, and it is powerful. He gets a lot of the physical touch he needs at a time when I can offer it freely (unlike, say, at dinnertime or when I am packing lunches). He practices fine and gross motor skills under my supervision and encouragement—a rarity in a very busy household. We celebrate when he does big things and breathe through the frequent frustrations. There is a spirituality in dressing a toddler. I hope you find it, too.

Mealtimes

Mealtimes, even though they can be fraught with frustrations and refusals, are another powerful routine. In fact, research indicates that children with regular family mealtimes are less likely to become truant or drop out of school. A lot will change in their routine between the ages of one and four years, but keeping some consistency is warranted. A valuable reminder is that their metabolism gets used to a timely, regular meal. That means that tempers can flare as their blood sugar dips around expected mealtimes. I'll provide you with plenty of mealtime tips and tricks in the coming chapters, but in general, it is a smart investment to hold family mealtimes sacred.

DISCIPLINE

It is best to think of discipline as *teaching* and not strictly as *punishment*. Linguistically, discipline is a word used to describe the way one approaches a *disciple*. It connotes the relationship between teacher and student. When I speak of discipline, I am not speaking strictly about punishments. I am talking about the careful use of affirmations, encouragement, consequences, and rewards in order to shape behavior and learning. It may be best to think of discipline as a kind of impassioned discipleship rather than an authoritarian use of force.

It can be hard to know the best way to discipline your toddler in the heat of a moment. The right choice depends on the situation, your child, and the targeted behavior. Even if you have studied and memorized all the best practices of effective parents, getting it right every time is impossible. That said, there are things that you can do that will make you more effective more of the time. You can create value-driven responses, practice them, and introduce disciplinary moments that don't cause disconnection. It is possible to yell less and stay connected during tough, teaching moments. *Connected, nurturing discipline is possible.*

We will do a lot of reflection and intention-setting in part 2. You'll be offered exercises that help you stay calm, increase your understanding, and deepen your connection to your child. In general, the best discipline is *prevention*. Believe it or not, there are a lot of wonderful things you can do to prevent behavioral problems and avoid disciplinary action. When parents think of discipline as *teaching* and use all the tools in their discipline tool belt (not just punishment), the world opens, and family life becomes easier. Peace becomes possible, and relationships strengthen.

What follows in this section is a review of every toddler parent's big three: tantrums, timeouts, and spanking. I will also introduce you to plans for helping you stay calm and keep calm during tough moments. As strange (or frustrating!) as this might sound, it is a very deep truth: *All successful discipline begins with parent self-control.*

Tantrums

People associate tantrums with toddlers more than any other behavior during this phase of development. I believe that a toddler's ability to make nuclear-level messes should be the more pervasive discussion. There is *nothing in this world* more startling than walking into your living room to find a quiet toddler holding an open Sharpie. I also feel like the good far outweighs the bad in this stage of life. Toddlers are awesome bundles of curiosity, learning, and  the best cuddles you'll ever receive. Regardless of how I may feel, tantrums are the highlight of most parenting lore. I am sure this is due to the tantrum's unique ability to stir caregivers into a frenzy of fear, concern, and confusion. Peanut butter always gets associated with jelly, and young children can't escape their reputation for explosive outbursts (and the seemingly inconsequential reasons that trigger them). For many of you, the handling of tantrums is a key concern.

In order to easily and compassionately intervene, it helps to know a few general things about tantrums. Then we can use this foundational knowledge to build our connection-driven responses in part 2.

What Happens During Tantrums?

Here is a typical tantrum: Happy child wants milk. Mother pours milk in blue cup. Toddler pours milk on floor. Toddler screams that milk should have been served in the red cup that family doesn't even own.

Tantrums like this occur when the child's developing brain dis-integrates; that is, the parts of the brain that are learning to think, plan, and be logical stop communicating with the parts of the brain that are experiencing big emotions. This process is biologically predetermined and a part of normal development. *It is not the result of a child being "bad."* We call it dis-integration, or the loss of integration between important parts of the brain.

Tantrums are the result of an undeveloped prefrontal cortex that is *both* underresourced and underexperienced to deal with the gigantic (and disappointing) realities of the toddler's world. The toddler is increasingly aware that they are separate from their parents, and they are driven to exert their independence.

In the preceding example, the toddler's strange reaction (the tantrum-like behavior) might be understood as a poor, but typical, adaptation to the relatively new experience of having preferences, stating demands, or wanting change. As strange as it sounds, the brain has to learn to deal with the co-mingling of power and preference. Feminist literature might call this the fledgling use of "voice," a sentiment that I think is both spot-on and beautiful. Toddlers are also developing language skills to express their ideas, feelings, wants, and needs. Sometimes their expressive language lags behind their feelings or wants, which is *incredibly* frustrating: "I don't have the language to express my disappointment, so I will pour this milk on the ground."

Neurologically, their capacities for self-control, waiting, and coping won't fully develop until their mid-twenties. The beginning of this brain-growth period, which is obviously kick-started in the toddler years, is quite painful. The brain is easily derailed and dis-regulated. What looks like a typical meltdown resembles an electrical storm in the brain that can be watched like a movie on an MRI. For many toddlers, the tantrum is as much neurological as it is behavioral.

The toddler's desire to express their independence, or perhaps their inability to express their disappointment, can become very big very quickly. Because their brain is unpracticed at expressing preferences and their verbal skills are still developing, the part of the brain that experiences emotions easily swallows up the part of the brain that is calm, logical, and verbal. Again, this display is evidence of normal development and not indicative of an ill-tempered nature.

What Causes Tantrums?

As the brain is growing and developing important self-regulatory capacities, there are several things parents can do to equip children for success with managing their tempers. Your child's brain is working harder right now than it will at any other stage of development. I find it helpful to think of my job as a kind of personal trainer, chef, and sleep coach for an endurance athlete. I want them to succeed, but I also know that they need to be well prepared for the day's work (in this case, the work of making those neural connections). The best way to be a proactive parent who sets up their little growth-monster for success is to HALT. HALT—an acronym for Hungry, Angry, Lonely, or Tired—helps a parent remember to notice when a child is becoming testy or restless and ask four important questions:

* **Is my child hungry?** Keep healthy, protein-rich snacks available and make sure to keep your child's sugar intake at a minimum. Some foods can even cause agitated behavior—certain food dyes, for example. Keep an eye out and intervene!
* **Is my child angry?** If you wonder whether your child is feeling a big emotion or having trouble verbalizing a need, step in. Make a habit of using emotion words in conversation, such as "I wonder if you're feeling angry. I can see that your hands are tense, and your shoulders are up by your ears." Encourage body movement in ways that release muscle tension.
* **Is my child lonely?** Sometimes children feel disconnected from us, perhaps because they have had a tough day or because we're distracted. Put away your phone or tell whomever you are with that you need just five minutes to connect with your little one. Join in your toddler's play or ask if they want to sit in your lap for a bit. Spending a lot of time together before leaving the house or before introducing them to new situations can be surprisingly helpful.

* **Is my child tired?** Fatigue is major, major, MAJOR. If you have missed a nap, reconsider the rest of your day or plan for a meltdown by telling yourself that you won't take it personally and that you will make time to console your child when things get rough (because they will). If your child is very tired, don't expect to introduce new people or novel situations with ease. They are running on fumes. It isn't surrender to simply suggest a quiet activity like coloring or a movie.

What to Do During Tantrums

There are many ideas about the best way to intervene during a tantrum. I am going to quickly spell out some general truths about tantrum intervention. There are a lot of exercises in this book, divided according to the age of your child, to help you create meaningful interventions that work for you. But for now, here are a few quick and easy rules that always apply:

* **Stay calm.** The key to all successful parenting—and most certainly to effective intervention during tantrums—is parental *self-control*. We will review some more practical steps to make it easier for you to keep your cool in the exercises following part 2.
* **Ask yourself why.** Considering the motivation for the behavior can be very helpful. It might be helpful to reframe the question as "What is my child struggling with?"
* **Empathize with the child's feelings.** The feelings are never the problem; it is what the child is doing with those feelings that can become problematic. Acknowledging the feelings, without judgment, is a great first step.
* **Ignore the behavior, not the child.** A lot of times, it is very effective to ignore the tantrum. The trick is to first communicate that you are available, loving, and patient but that you're not going to participate in the tantrum. Connection is the key. "I can see that you're very angry. I am sorry. I am going to make dinner now, and I hope that you will help me once you have calmed down."
* **Be consistent.** Many parents create rules on the fly and react quickly when things go wrong, which leaves little room for forethought and makes consistency very hard. The goal, however, is to try to make similar choices in similar

situations and to hold relatively consistent boundaries. Trust that creating space for planning and forethought is a priority because consistency is a very helpful intervention (and prevention) for tantrums.

✴ **Offer alternatives.** If your toddler's goals are acceptable, help them find more appropriate means to achieve them. If your child is full of energy and won't stop running in the house, let them run outside with your supervision. If they are angry and throwing things, help them find safer ways to express the anger in their bodies, like stomping their feet or throwing pillows. There are healthy, non-hurtful ways to express emotions.

Timeouts

Timeouts have been getting a bad rap lately, which is a major problem for many parents because timeouts are the single most common form of discipline. This is one of those topics about which I hear tons of misinformation. Many exasperated moms complain, "My kid's behavior is terrible, and we are both so mad, but since I can't use timeouts anymore, I don't know what to do." Me: blank stare.

Very few people in my position actually advocate for the cessation of timeouts. This is one of those things that parents misinterpret when they read a quick article title and move on. Timeouts are fine, but they are *nuanced*. It is true that timeouts can be done very poorly, but they can also be an invaluable tool of parental self-regulation and de-escalation.

When timeouts are approached with anger, shaming, and harsh disconnection (that is, as punishment), then timeouts are detrimental to the child. They cause a very distressed disconnection between parent and child that further increases the emotional upset. Plus, this way of using timeouts takes away the parent's valuable calm and control from the toddler at a time when they so desperately need those influences. When they are in the middle of chaos (a tantrum), they need your calm.

There are times, however, when children are so out of control that they cannot accept comfort, or they become increasingly agitated by any effort to intervene. There are also times when the parent senses their own loss of control and can no longer be rational and calm. When emotions are this high, a break for both the parent and the child is a healthy solution. When timeouts are used to give the child and the adult a break, to prevent further escalation, and to give everyone a chance to regain control, then timeouts are a powerful positive parenting solution. You can come back together when you are both calm and are able to problem-solve effectively.

If you continue to struggle with timeouts, here are a few tips:

* **Create a safe space.** Talk to the child in advance about a place in the house that everyone can use to de-escalate. Explain to them ahead of time that when they are sent to the special corner (or even when they choose to go there), no one is in trouble, and everyone is still loved.
* **Choose an appropriate time limit.** Usually three to five minutes is appropriate, then you can go back and check on them. Ideally, you would end the break when the child is calm, but if this isn't possible, use the time to de-escalate all other parties (including yourself) and keep checking in.
* **Keep expectations in check.** If your child is younger than three years, they won't be using the timeout to reflect on what they have done. Don't use it in this way. The timeout, especially for young toddlers, is instead a way to help them learn to cope with strong emotions in a safe space.

Staying Calm

The beginning of all effective discipline is parental self-control, thoughtfulness, and intention. You absolutely cannot teach your child self-control if you have none. You cannot give your child peace, gentleness, and respect if you have none. That is why part 2 includes opportunities to practice various calming techniques. They will come in handy when you transition into more complicated teaching moments that require your self-control and thoughtfulness. In these moments, your level-headed calm will be a critical asset.

Toddler parenting is hard. It is natural to be aggravated and have your patience tested. That's why it's wise to simply get in the habit of using calming techniques regularly. When your child turns two and tests their limits (and your temper) at every turn, you'll be grateful that you took time to create habits for yourself that clear your mind, help you recover from emotional upset, and keep you mindfully aware of your parenting values.

How to Create a Calming Practice

Developmental psychologists love to remind us that "those things that fire together, wire together." By this, they mean that those actions that are done frequently together or in sequence with one another (*fire together*) bind together neurologically in a unique way (*wire together*). If you always have a fizzy drink with pizza, then you will crave a fizzy drink every time you have pizza.

A more useful example is meditation and self-calming. When you take time to practice calming techniques regularly, especially when they aren't necessarily needed, then those resources will be readily available to you when they're necessary. That is because practice truly does affect your brain's architecture. Through practice (*fire together*), we bind simple actions like breathing, reflection, and counting to more complex feelings like calm, thoughtfulness, or peacefulness (*wire together*). This makes these things that are traditionally more difficult to initiate (like a calm sense of thoughtful well-being) readily accessible because we have already done the daily work.

Choose two or three times throughout the day when you can practice a calming technique for up to 10 minutes. It might be during your commute, in the shower, while you're making dinner, or during a separate moment of stillness. Stillness (or distraction-free quiet) isn't necessary, but it may be helpful at first.

WHAT IS THE GOAL?

The goal of effective calming strategies isn't total happiness and satisfaction. Life is still happening; circumstances can be difficult. With any calming strategy, the goal should be persistence and mindful awareness. If we can't get to a happy place, then we certainly can aim for feelings that are easier to practice. Try moving in the direction of one or more of the following feelings:

ASSURED AWARE CALM
CAUTIOUS CONFIDENT CONTENT
CURIOUS ENCOURAGING FULL
GENTLE GRACIOUS GRATEFUL
HOPEFUL INSPIRED KIND LOVING
OBSERVANT SATISFIED SOFT
SUPPORTIVE WISE

THE FIVE R'S OF BRAIN BUILDING

The quality of a child's early experiences with you is THE powerhouse ingredient in your child's learning trajectory. The five most important tools in your tool belt are relationship, respect, repetition, routines, and responsive interactions.

Zero to Three, which is one of those powerhouse research institutions that is changing the world, calls these five tools the 5 R's of Brain Building. Let's see them again:

* Relationship
* Respect
* Repetition
* Routines
* Responsive interactions

The 5 R's are a guidepost for most of the exercises throughout the rest of this book. By establishing strong intentions early in your parenting journey, you can begin structuring a life for your family that is always considering these elements and finding ways to build upon these strongholds. Being intentional is one of the first and very best steps toward meeting your parenting goals, supporting your child's needs, and laying a strong foundation for all future development.

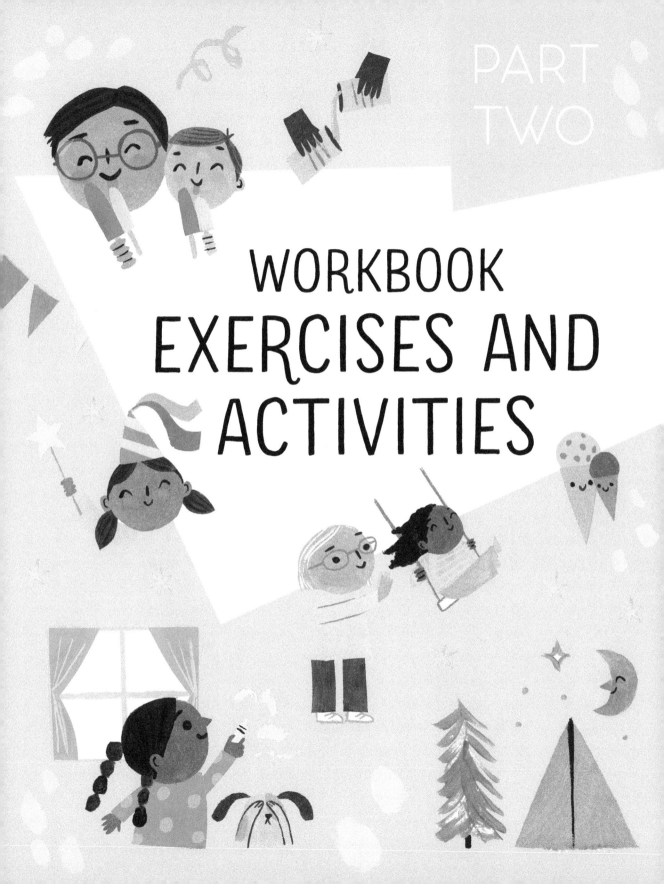

WORKBOOK
EXERCISES AND
ACTIVITIES

CHAPTER ONE

12
MONTH-OLDS

At 12 months of age, children start to feel less like babies. The infancy stage is officially over, and "the toddling" either has begun or is about to begin. Let's review a brief picture of where your child's motor skills, language skills, and thinking skills are at this stage.

12-MONTH-OLD MILESTONES

Developmental milestones are the individual skills that children master while they grow physically, intellectually, and emotionally. They typically occur in a predictable sequence and timeline, but this isn't always the case. Remember, the range for normal development is quite wide. So, don't worry if your children aren't perfectly on pace with the general guideline or if one child outpaces another. Use your child's wellness visits with the pediatrician to discuss any concerns you may have about your toddler, and if you have a preemie, don't forget to use their adjusted age.

Gross Motor Muscles

Walking: At first your child will work on *standing* (9.5–14 months), and then *cruising*, which is walking while holding onto furniture (7–13 months). Then they will begin *walking alone* (11–15 months), and finally they will start *running* (13–20 months). Hold on to your hat!

Fine Motor Muscles

Hand and finger coordination: Your child should already be reaching, pointing, and grabbing, but soon they should start *banging two objects together* (7–12 months). Then they should start trying to grab things between the thumb and forefinger. This is known as the *"pincer grasp"* (9–14 months). They should start *putting things inside containers* (10–14 months) and *scribbling* on anything you put in front of them (11–16 months).

Eating: Are you ready for food fun? Soon your toddler will start *bringing a cup to their mouth* (10–17 months) and using a fork and spoon correctly (13–20 months).

Language and Communication

Comprehension: At this age, your little one should start following simple directions (12–24 months) and responding consistently to your verbalizations and the emotions in your voice.

Expression: Your child's expressive language is about to explode! They can say "Mama" or "Dada" with purpose (9–14 months), then add an additional three words (11.5–21 months), and then another six words (14–21 months), and then go completely bananas at right around 2 years. They can point and grunt with purpose to show you what they want or need (10–15 months), and they should start being articulate enough for strangers to recognize a few words around 17 months.

Social and Emotional

Your child is learning what to expect from others based on interactions and experiences with parents and caregivers. They are also developing a sense of self. *They are learning who they are and what they can expect.* They do not yet have the capacity for impulse control. Punishing them for not exhibiting self-control or restraint is little more than a shame-based tactic as the parts of the brain that inhibit behaviors are underdeveloped. They can play ball with another person and shake their head "no." They may even begin symbolic play with a doll (for example, pretend feeding) at this age.

Intelligence

Their intellectual development at this age is very simple. Their problem-solving skills are just starting to show. The most obvious test might be hiding an object (under a cup or behind your back) and noticing that they will now search for it.

WALKERS VERSUS TALKERS

There is an important note about the funny way the toddler's brain seems to budget its limited energy and resources. Typically, children will work on either language development or motor skill development. For whatever reason, it is rare that both of these areas develop completely sequentially and simultaneously. Typically, a child who is working very hard on the crawling, standing, and walking sequence will slow down (or even stop) their verbalizations. It is as though the brain presses pause in the language centers while the motor cortex is hard at work (or vice versa). My daughter is an excellent example of this. She was singing and speaking in full sentences (language skills) a little after her first birthday but didn't attempt to hold a fork (fine motor skills) until she was almost three. As her vocabulary continued to explode, her handwriting was that of a tired (and maybe visually impaired) serial killer. Just now, at six years old, everything seems to be on pace together. It took a while for all the areas of her brain to get into lockstep.

ℓℓ WELLNESS ℓℓ

At 12 months of age, wellness is about those critical routines, like sleep and play, as well as healthy nutrition. One thing that often gets overlooked but is also very important to child well-being at this stage is healthy attachment relationships. Healthy attachment relationships are those that are consistent, warm, attuned, and responsive to the child's needs and temperament. In the following chapters, we will emphasize the skills of temperament recognition (that is, helping your child feel seen and known) and the skills of attunement. But, for now, I want to help you think about smart ways to introduce new foods and the best ways to facilitate healthy attachments.

I have also included a brief screening quiz for parental depression. The reason for this is because patterns of relationship (how children form attachments) develop over the first few years of life and can influence mental health and wellness throughout childhood. Caregivers struggling with overwhelming problems, such as depression, may be less able to effectively attune to and respond to their children during this critical period. At this stage, *your ability to pay attention, notice needs, and respond appropriately really matters.*

DETERMINING IMPORTANT ADULTS

We need to help very young toddlers build strong, positive bonds with important adults. What seems obvious can be difficult in a busy world filled with distracted adults. The parents are the most important adults, but there are other adults who matter as well. They might be day care workers, grandparents, or any other person who the toddlers see routinely. Important adults are people who the child might regularly depend on for some level of sustenance, support, protection, or care.

Who are your child's other important adults? Let's make a list! Take a moment to think about it; we want this list to be thorough. Also note each adult's role in the child's life and the setting in which they typically engage your child. I've added an example to start you out.

Name	Role	Setting
Sandra	*Afternoon caregiver*	*Day care facility*

STRENGTHENING THE BOND

When children this age create secure attachments to important adults, they show more positive emotion and less anxiety (maybe throw fewer tantrums) in early childhood, and they have an easier time establishing relationships with peers at school. The best way to build secure attachments is to ensure relative consistency and to help these important adults be responsive. The single, hands-down, best way to do that is to *collaborate with caregivers.*

Fill out the following information to share with these important adults. We want them to learn from you about your child. I want you to start this important conversation about your child's temperament and preferences with them so that they, too, feel comfortable sharing with you what they are learning about your child. You never know: Your babysitter might have finally found a way to get your child to eat their peas or have discovered a certain song that soothes them!

IMPORTANT INFORMATION ABOUT MY CHILD

If I had to describe my toddler in two sentences, I would say:

_____

_____

_____

Likes and dislikes

My child's favorite toys	Things my child does *not* like	Things my child likes	My child's favorite activities

Here are a few things that work to CALM my child:

_____

_____

_____

Here are a few things that UPSET my child:

_____

_____

_____

Other important conversation starters:

✳ My child's treasured routines are:

_____

_____

_____

✳ My child's favorite foods are:

_____

_____

_____

✳ My child's preferred names and labels for valued objects and people are:

_____

_____

_____

✱ The schedule that typically works best for my child is:

_____

_____

_____

DEPRESSION SCREENING

The depression you may be experiencing at this stage of a child's life is unique in that shame provides an undercurrent for much of the experience. The truth: Postpartum depression (PPD) is relatively common but goes undetected as often as 50 percent of the time. The worst cases make their way into news stories and memoirs, while we don't hear about the more moderate experiences of postpartum sadness, confusion, and apathy.

Following is a quick and easy quiz to help you identify what (if any) symptoms of depression you may be experiencing. Whether or not you have a diagnosis isn't nearly as important as understanding the symptoms and speaking to someone about them.

Take the following quiz. All questions represent PPD symptoms and *are not* normal parts of motherhood. Even if you only answer "yes" to one question, talk to your doctor or a friend. Suffering shouldn't be a typical part of parenting. All you have to do is look a trusted person in the eye and force yourself to say, "I am struggling." Your toddler deserves this single act of great courage.

I have not been able to laugh and see the funny side of things lately.	Yes	No	Not Sure
I haven't looked forward to things with enjoyment nearly as much as I used to.	Yes	No	Not Sure
Most of the time, when things go wrong, I feel like I only have myself to blame.	Yes	No	Not Sure
Friends and family seem to think that I shouldn't be worrying about the things that I worry about.	Yes	No	Not Sure
I feel scared and panicky a lot of the time. Even though the fear feels very real, my friends and family think I have no reason to be scared.	Yes	No	Not Sure
I am having more trouble coping lately. I feel agitated, angry, weepy, or over-whelmed a lot of the time.	Yes	No	Not Sure
Even though my baby is sleeping, I don't seem to be able to stay asleep. I wake up on and off throughout the night. Sometimes I have thoughts that keep me awake; sometimes I don't know why I can't sleep.	Yes	No	Not Sure
I feel sad and miserable a lot of the time.	Yes	No	Not Sure
I have been so sad or worried that I cry a lot of the time.	Yes	No	Not Sure
The thought of harming myself has crossed my mind a few times lately.	Yes	No	Not Sure
I have unwanted or intrusive thoughts.	Yes	No	Not Sure

FEEDING FOR HEALTH AND WELL-BEING

Many young toddlers are still quite instinctual about the foods they desire, and their choices often reflect their body's nutritional demands at that moment. It is illuminating to watch your child reject veggies but eat all their protein in the morning and then reverse that impulse in the evening. Supporting these instincts can help your child avoid obesity by reinforcing a smart, intuitive approach to their body's nutritional demands.

The best way to support this kind of food exploration and intuitive eating is to offer four food groups at every single meal. Those four food categories are:

* Protein
* Vegetables
* Fruit
* Carbohydrates

Be careful to introduce only one new food item a day so that you can monitor your child for allergies or food sensitivities. After each introduction, watch throughout the following hours or days for flushing, diarrhea, increased fussiness, and eczema.

Following are several suggestions for food items in each category that children this age often enjoy. They are also easy to prepare ahead, store in individual containers, and pull out at each meal for several days in a row. Use the two right columns to note when you introduce the food and any observations you make. You can also write recipe ideas or other foods you would like to try on the lines that follow each table.

PROTEIN

Type of food	Date served	Observation
Cut-up string cheese or shredded cheese		
Eggs, scrambled or hard-boiled		
Lunch meat, cut into squares		
Canned black beans		
Shredded and diced pot roast		

VEGETABLES

Type of food	Date served	Observation
Cooked carrots		
Peas		
Green beans		
Cooked broccoli		
Baked and cubed squash		
Baked and cubed sweet potato		

_____

_____

_____

FRUIT

Type of food	Date served	Observation
Applesauce		
Cut-up grapes		
Canned mandarin oranges		
Sliced strawberries		
Bananas		
Kiwi		

CARBOHYDRATES

Type of food	Date served	Observation
Whole-wheat bowtie pasta		
Torn quesadillas		
Potato latkes		
Corn bread		
Oatmeal or grits		

_____

_____

_____

Pinterest.com can be an excellent resource for meal planning and food introductions. You can enhance the activity in this section by plugging search terms into Pinterest. For example, try "easy toddler meals," "feeding schedule for 12-month-old," and "toddler recipes."

LEARNING

Everything you need to know can be said in three words: follow their lead. Learning is all about slowing down, minimizing your distractions, getting excited when they are excited, supporting (but not eliminating) optimal frustrations, and paying attention to what they are interested in. It is about noticing what they notice, labeling things, and helping them reach, build, and speak. Your jobs are simply to support their exploration and independence, be a safe base to which they can return without punishment or repercussion, and offer comfort, rest, and adequate boundaries. These things make them feel secure enough to learn.

The exercises in this chapter will help you support learning in two areas: (1) literacy and language and (2) thinking and problem solving. We start building social and emotional competencies such as self-control, compassion, and sharing in chapter 2. Feel free to jump ahead if you like. It is never too early to begin thinking about these things, even if it is just helpful background noise.

LEARNING ACTIVITIES CHECKLIST

In this exercise, I have provided a simplified checklist of learning activities to try with your child. Then, in the next exercise, I have provided a blank calendar to help you plan the next month. Read (and maybe reread) the list first. I think that when you really consider these activities you will get a general sense of the kinds of experiences and interactions that help 12- to 18-month-old children thrive. This should help you be creative in the future.

If you already feel confident in a particular activity, place a check mark in the box beside the suggestion. At the end of your reading, you should be able to quickly scan through the list to know in what areas you might need support or additional learning.

- [ ] Name the people, places, and things that your child sees.
- [ ] Sing together and make up rhymes and stories.
  (*Pinterest: "nursery rhymes"*)
- [ ] Help your child practice sorting. (*Pinterest: "sorting fun"*)
- [ ] Cook some spaghetti, prepare yourself for a mess, and let your child play with it.
- [ ] Work on a three- or four-piece puzzle or with building blocks. Encourage your child to solve problems, but don't do all the work for them. Be patient.
- [ ] Let your child hold and wave a bubble wand.
- [ ] Model longer sentences. For example, when your child says "milk" and points to the glass, respond with "You want more milk."
- [ ] Encourage scribbling. For example, tape a piece of paper to the tray of their high chair and then give them a crayon.
- [ ] Play simple games that involve following directions, like "Simon Says" or even "Pat-a-Cake." (*Pinterest: "games for babies"*)
- [ ] Encourage and support your children's efforts to do things for themselves.
- [ ] Introduce props like plastic dishes or a toy telephone that encourage pretend play.
- [ ] Join in and expand on your child's play. For example, if they stack two blocks, add a third. If they want to stomp their feet, encourage them to also clap their hands.
- [ ] Put your child's feelings into words. "I see that you're really mad that we quit reading." (*Pinterest: "feeling words"*)
- [ ] Build a sensory bin that provides tactile exploration opportunities for your child. (*Pinterest: "sensory bin"*)
- [ ] Support your child as they practice new skills. Provide *just enough* of the support they need to master a skill. Try to keep yourself from doing a difficult activity for them. Let them struggle a bit. Determine the least amount of intervention that would help them achieve their desired

goal. This can be tough for some parents. An example might be pointing to the location of a puzzle piece rather than taking the piece, orienting it correctly, and placing it in the right spot.

- ☐ Follow your child's interests.
- ☐ Talk about what you are doing together as you do it.
- ☐ Repeat the sounds and words your child uses to have back-and-forth interactions.
- ☐ Comment on what your child does well.
- ☐ Allow your child to practice drinking from a cup in an empty bathtub. (*Pinterest: "fine motor activities"*)
- ☐ Invite another toddler over to play.
- ☐ Encourage independent play. (*Pinterest: "independent toddler activities"*)
- ☐ Make a drum set out of pans and wooden spoons.
- ☐ Play running, jumping, and moving games like "Duck, Duck, Goose," "The Wheels on the Bus," and "The Hokey Pokey."
- ☐ Get down on your toddler's level to see what they see from their perspective.
- ☐ Make sure there are plenty of safe, low places to practice climbing.
- ☐ Provide a variety of toys that can be pushed and pulled.
- ☐ Take a trip to the park. (*Pinterest: "playground games"*)
- ☐ Give your child choices whenever possible. For example, "Do you want to eat your noodles or your fruit first? Do you want to wear blue pants or red pants?"
- ☐ Get down to your child's eye level to hug them.
- ☐ When your child makes help-seeking gestures such as reaching, grunting, or opening and closing their hand, say, "It looks like you need help. Here you go."

LEARNING ACTIVITIES CALENDAR

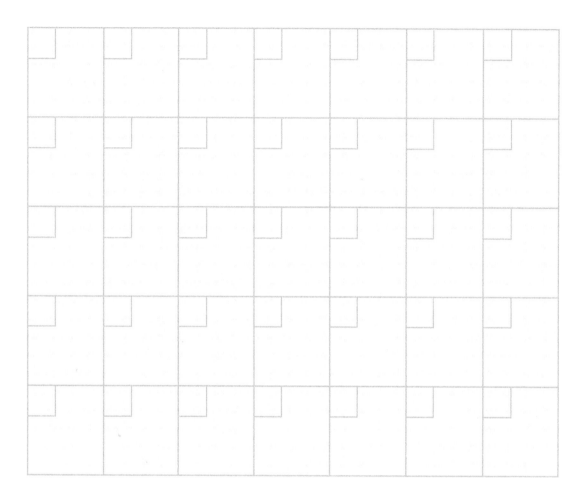

Use the calendar template above to distribute each of the 31 activities over the next month. Would I like you to do any and all of these activities all the time? Absolutely! But I know that you'll learn best and create valuable habits if you take time to focus on one each day for a whole month. They aren't activities that require preparation. Many are simply the foundational elements of good habits that you can practice one day at a time.

I promise that you'll be more attuned, feel more confident, and have a deeper understanding of optimal learning experiences at the end of the next month.

READING WITH YOUNG TODDLERS: POP QUIZ

Let's test your knowledge about best practices for reading with a very young toddler. Read through the following questions and make your best guess. At the end, I will tell you the answers. I know it is tempting to skip to the end and just read the right choices, but stopping to consider the best course of action is very helpful. Remember: *What fires together, wires together.* Using your imagination helps create a footprint for future instincts.

1. What is the best way to use the written word to enhance your 12- to 18-month-old child's language and literacy skills?

   A. Sitting across from them, looking them in the eyes, making frequent eye contact, and reading a great picture book
   B. Showing them flashcards of words with matching pictures
   C. Letting the child explore the book in whatever way they like, even if this means staying on the same page the whole time

2. What are the best books for a 12-month-old child?

   A. Simple ones with brightly colored designs and picture of things that are familiar to them
   B. Elaborate and exciting pop-up books
   C. Books with a compelling plot

3. Holding and cuddling a 12-month-old during reading time is too distracting and keeps them from acquiring new words.

   True / False

4. Copying your baby's sounds and encouraging them to repeat you is distracting and silly.

   True / False

5. The plot, words, rhyme scheme, and direction of a book are not that important when reading to a 12-month-old.

   True / False

6. Your child wants to read the same book every single day. What should you do?

   A. Refuse to read it. Reading the same book every day underexposes the child to new words and pictures.
   B. Read it again and again. Repetition strengthens the connections in the brain and helps them learn new skills
   C. Offer them another book. Novelty is critical to young toddlers and keeps them interested.

Answers:

1. **C.** It is best to let the child explore the book in whatever way they would like. I encourage you to have boundaries: "Uh oh! We don't tear pages. Let's use a more gentle touch to turn the pages." Offer chunky board books, soft books, or books that truly can be explored freely without seriously damaging them.

2. **A.** The very best books for 12-month-old children are simple, brightly colored books with pictures the child can relate to or that are familiar. They can be used to practice vocabulary. Notice the way your child interacts with each simple image and follow their lead.

3. **False.** Holding a child during the reading routine is powerful, brain-building stuff. It keeps them engaged, helps them feel loved, and makes them feel safe enough to learn from the process of reading.

4. **False.** When a child is cooing and making noises while reading, you can begin the back-and-forth of conversation: repeating the noise, noticing how they respond, waiting, and then offering another repetition until the "conversation" ends. If, however, the child is point to a cow and going "ca, ca, ca," then say "cow." Knowing the difference between fun babbling and vocalizations versus attempts at vocabulary acquisition is important.

5. **True.** When it comes to reading with a young toddler, your job is to follow their lead. Say the things and words that they point to, let them laugh and grunt at pages, or let them flip one or two (or no) pages. The plot doesn't matter.

6. **B.** Like loving and nonintrusive touching, repetition is critical to learning in this age group. Your child may say the same thing over and over or want to read the same book every night for weeks. It is okay to introduce new books, but if they aren't interested, don't push it.

BOUNDARIES AND ⟨⟨ ROUTINES ⟨⟨

Boundaries and routines with a 12- to 18-month-old are very important. You may remember from our discussion in part 1 that *routines* are imperative to all child learning and a critical part of healthy development. This is because routines contribute to the child's sense of safety. They also invite *repetition*, which is critical to brain-building. Plus, behavioral routines like teeth-brushing and physical activity can even influence long-term health. Let's start with play and sleep—two of your 12-month-old's most valuable routines.

Maybe you are not paying attention to your young toddler's routines because you are very busy or "going with the flow." You might also have your child in day care and simply not know much about their schedule during the day. That's okay. Skip to *Noticing Your Toddler's Schedule (see page 63)* in this section and begin there. Determining your child's schedule is as easy as making a record of their play, eat, and sleep times each day and then stepping back and noticing any patterns. Once you notice your child's typical metabolic patterns (when they are hungry) and sleep patterns, then you can begin to become more predictable and intentional about the routines discussed in the following sections. Predictability and intentionality are very important to creating the kinds of routines that facilitate your child's health and well-being.

PLAYTIME

Playtime is one of your child's most treasured routines. At this age, your child needs *a minimum* of four 20-minute periods of dedicated play with a responsive, valued caregiver. It is very important that you set aside several moments to stop what you are doing and engage your child in attuned, responsive play. You should also be playfully engaged when you are simply in the room with them but busy doing other things.

This exercise is an opportunity to expand on the skills that are most important during the dedicated playtime moments. We call this "floor time" because parents should be on the child's level.

In the *Learning Activities Checklist (see page 47)*, we established several ideas for play activities (because play is learning and learning is play at this age), but here we will work specifically to strengthen *your skills* so that your play routines can have the maximum impact. The simple skills for great play are:

- ✳ Watch and wait
- ✳ Follow the leader
- ✳ Take turns
- ✳ Get moving
- ✳ Solve problems
- ✳ Leave them alone

WATCH AND WAIT

Notice what your child is trying to do, and either offer them just enough support for them to achieve their goal or encourage them to take the next step toward a new goal.

Bring to mind your most recent observation of your child's play. What skills are they working on? (For example, are they stacking, sorting, climbing, or reaching?)

_____

_____

How can you help them achieve their goal without doing it yourself? The goal is *their* self-esteem and mastery, not *yours*.

_____

_____

FOLLOW THE LEADER

Not all kids play the same way. Some kids want a lot of stimulation and noise, while others are more easily overwhelmed. You need to follow their lead.

How can you tell when your child is excited, curious, or interested? (For example, are they clapping, grunting, pointing, smiling, or bouncing?) Be descriptive.

_____

_____

How can you tell when your child is bored or needs stimulation?

_____

_____

How can you tell when your child is overwhelmed, overstimulated, or fatigued with an activity? (Are they crying, yawning, turning their head, or moving away?)

_____

_____

TAKE TURNS

Play back-and-forth games. Mimic their behavior and noises, and then wait for a response. Explore an item together in a similar way.

What are some ways that you might take turns with your young toddler? Specifically consider the way your child plays, the things they enjoy, or the skills they are working on.

_____

_____

GET MOVING

Create safe spaces where your young toddler can move, roll, walk, climb, and explore with all their senses freely. If you live in a museum, that's okay, but your toddler needs safe spaces, too.

Consider your home or your child's place of care. What can be done to make the space safe enough that you don't feel like you have to monitor, restrict, or discipline during play?

_____

_____

SOLVE PROBLEMS

Problem-solving activities are things like stacking blocks, stringing beads, fitting cups into each other, and putting Cheerios in a water bottle.

What kinds of activities could you do regularly and on special occasions that can help you and your toddler explore how things move, fit, and work together?

_____

_____

_____

LEAVE THEM ALONE

Young toddlers need a lot of interaction. They also need to play independently sometimes. You have things to do, and it is okay for your toddler to explore.

Honestly, how does it feel to see your toddler practicing independence? For some parents, it is a relief; for others, it is tough.

_____

_____

Is there a place in your house where your child can play independently—perhaps on the floor beside you while you cook dinner—where you feel comfortable being distracted? Jot down a couple of places or activities that will keep your child interested while you accomplish your own tasks.

_____

_____

A NOTE ABOUT KEEPING BROAD BOUNDARIES AND EXPECTATIONS

Boundaries, which are composed of both expectations and limits, should not be relegated to the realm of "parenting style" and opinion. Boundaries are actually very important to growth and learning. When boundaries are done well, they reflect the family's values and communicate those values through gentle, nonjudgmental guidance. Saying with a smiling face and a happy voice, "Uh-oh! We don't pull all the books off of the shelf. I'll have to keep stopping you until you can stop yourself," communicates to children that your family values cleanliness and respects space.

Boundaries also establish *expectations*. In this example, the expectation is that your child will one day abstain from pulling everything off shelves. Once your child masters certain skills, they can feel great about meeting your expectations. In fact, this process of creating expectations and gently supporting your child until they can meet them is foundational to self-esteem.

At 12 months, when your child has little self-control, you can establish an expectation for cleanliness while also communicating an understanding that "You aren't quite there yet, so I will keep helping you" or "You can't do this for yourself. I will do it for you until you can."

Broad expectations are very appropriate at this age. They include things like exploration, creativity, and curiosity rather than things like making the bed, dressing themselves, or feeding the dog. Narrow expectations like these are fine for older kids, but a 12-month-old is not ready for those yet. When your child exhibits curiosity (which is expected at this age), it should be a cause for celebration. Plus, you should still be able to place these broad expectations inside a firm boundary: "I see how curious you are about what is on this table, but you can't really see it, can you? We can't pull things down like that, so I will pick you up and help you find a better way to explore."

Gentle expectations that lay the foundation for the future enjoyment of mastery, mixed with firm boundaries that keep children safe and communicate values, are wonderful things to give your very young toddler.

SLEEP ROUTINE

Another critical routine is sleep. For children ages 12 months to 4 years, adequate sleep is critical for learning, behavior management, and clear thinking. Without sleep, toddlers misbehave and struggle with their inhibitions and temper.

The first and most important step is making sure your toddler has a quiet, safe, and predictable sleeping area in each of their significant environments. Once that has been secured, we can consider the necessary amount of sleep and the sleep schedule for children in this age range.

Write your child's typical daily sleep schedule in the following box. When are their typical morning wake times, nap times (and durations), and bedtimes? If you're having trouble with this, skip to the next exercise and come back to this in a few days.

Is your child's sleep schedule different at home than in their daily group care setting? If so, how?

_____

_____

When routines are very different between home and day care, children can feel stressed, confused, and anxious. When children are feeling confused, they can doubt their own security, competence, and confidence, which can challenge their ability to learn new skills.

How can you work to keep your child's sleep schedule more consistent? Remember, like all other valued routines, the sleep routine helps a child feels safe. What accommodations must be made to support it?

_____

_____

_____

_____

Many day care facilities consolidate multiple naps into one when the child becomes a toddler. This can be very difficult for children who still need two naps and come home exhausted, grumpy, or tearful. In that situation, I suggest moving the bedtime up, sometimes even to 6 p.m. Consistency is very helpful, so being accommodating in a way that honors your child's needs and offers predictability is wise.

SLEEP REQUIREMENTS FOR
12- TO 18-MONTH-OLDS

- Your child should be sleeping 10 to 12 hours each night plus taking two naps per day for a total additional 2 to 3 hours.
- Young toddlers should have two naps. Most don't drop to one nap until 16 to 18 months.
- Young toddlers should be asleep no later than 8 p.m. every night. Their nighttime sleep routine should initiate and end at approximately the same time every night and every morning.

Here is a typical and appropriate sleep schedule for a 12- to 18-month-old child.

7:00 a.m.	Wake
10:00/10:30 a.m.	Morning nap (at least one hour)
3:00/3:30 p.m.	Afternoon nap (at least one hour)
7:30 p.m.	Begin bedtime routine
8:00 p.m.	Be asleep by this time

NOTICING YOUR TODDLER'S SCHEDULE

This exercise is for parents who are new to being intentional about routines and scheduling. Write down (or have your child's caregiver write down) a note about the times your child engages each of the following routines: **play**, **sleep**, **wake**, and **eat**.

DAY:	
Time	Activity

DAY:	
Time	Activity

DAY:	
Time	Activity

Now, do the Sleep Routine exercise (see page 60), completing the first question with a rough estimate of the schedule that you think best fits your child at this time.

DISCIPLINE

The beginning of all effective discipline is parental self-control, thoughtfulness, and intention. At 12 to 18 months, when a child's ability to inhibit their behavior has not yet developed, there is no real necessity to discipline them for any reason. You can express boundaries and celebrate target behaviors—but scolding them for developmentally appropriate behaviors like wandering and mess-making should *not* be something a parent does at this stage. It is appropriate to prohibit certain behaviors by offering simple course correction or redirection, but anger about your child's poor self-control should be off the table.

Remember, discipline is much closer to the word "discipleship" than it is punishment. And yet punishment is the word most parents closely associate with discipline. From zero to three years of age, it is especially important that we make sure all our discipline is rooted in teaching, connection, and care. During this time, while your child might be coloring on the walls and throwing food on the floor, make connection your priority. Always share your expectations for their behavior in a way that expresses a benevolent understanding about both their limitations and their desires.

As promised, here's your first opportunity to practice a calming technique. Discipline must begin with your own self-control. For many parents, self-control is actually the hardest part. If you are one of them, I hope this tiny parallel gives you empathy for your child's lack of self-control.

CALMING TECHNIQUE:
TAKE THREE DEEP, CENTERING BREATHS

1. Sit with your back straight and body relaxed, resting your hands gently on your knees or beside you. You can close your eyes if you like.
2. Take a big breath in through your nose, filling your belly with air.
3. Slowly exhale through your mouth.
4. As you exhale, say "One" and relax your forehead and face.
5. Take another deep breath in through your nose and exhale through your mouth.
6. Say "Two" on the exhale and relax your shoulders and hands.
7. Take a third deep breath in through your nose and exhale through your mouth, saying "Three," and relax your belly and ribs.

How was this experience? If it helped you connect to the moment, breathe slower, or feel more relaxed, make a note of it:

_____

_____

_____

When will you practice this calming technique over the next week? Consider your to-dos for each day and find a certain time (upon waking, before falling asleep, while preparing meals or driving to work, and so forth) when this practice could be incorporated. You can even set a repeating reminder in your smartphone to prompt you to take those three deep breaths.

CHAPTER TWO

18

MONTH-OLDS

Many parents say this next stage (ages 18 to 24 months) was one of their favorite because their child really "came alive" in fun, interactive, and unexpected ways.

18-MONTH-OLD MILESTONES

18 months. That is a year and a half! Can you believe it? When my children were this age, my mother would often say, "The days are long, but the months are short." I couldn't have agreed more. Your child is active and babbling, fun and engaging, but still quite needy and, therefore, tiring. But it's a joyful exhaustion, and at times I even miss it. Your child is so lively, and their personality is solidifying in fun and unique ways every day. It can be difficult to keep up with the rapidity of their changing preferences and needs, and every day can feel like a new challenge (or perhaps a new adventure).

I am reluctant to dive too deeply into milestones at this age because there is just *so much variation* among children ages 12 to 18 months. I can mention a few things that might be red flags if not accomplished, but during a time when child-to-child comparison is such a painful journey for many mothers, I think it is best to hold these milestones loosely.

Enjoy the unique pace at which your child is developing. Some children are running at this age; others are carefully steadying each small step. Some children are speaking several words at this age; others are babbling indeterminately. As you read through the milestones, in this section in particular, try not to worry. I don't want anything to steal your gratitude and joy from this magical time with your 18-month-old.

Gross Motor Skills

These children are everywhere. The old expression "a bull in a china shop" couldn't be more apt. They walk, and many even climb. What is worse, they have enough coordination to move their arms *while they walk*. Which is to say, they can pull things off tables and shelves while they are mid-stride.

Fine Motor Skills

Hopefully your child is getting competent with their eating utensils and their cup. Before you freak out because your kid isn't holding their fork, get them naked and let them experiment by eating applesauce with a spoon or drinking from an open cup. Their abilities, however messy, might surprise you!

Language and Communication

Your child's receptive language will continue to move forward and likely outpace their expressive language. This means tantrums, biting, hitting, and all that other fun stuff. It helps to know that their language discrepancies make a lot of this kind of behavior quite normal.

There is quite a range in expressive language at this age, but if your child isn't saying at least six words or can't express themselves by shaking their head or gesturing, then you probably should speak to your doctor. But all other variation in expressive language is normal. In fact, *variation is normal.*

Social and Emotional

Trouble behaviors start to crop up in shocking ways at this age. A toddler's desire for autonomy waxes and wanes, and so do their tantrums. They have limited speech but awesome new motor skills, which means they are starting to use behavior to communicate—sometimes in big ways. It is best if you understand that biting and hitting are normal at this age. You can try to keep them from performing these behaviors by closely watching for signs of agitation, using gentle redirection, or even physically moving their body (for example, carefully holding their arm away from your face if they are hitting). Remind them that you can't let them engage in these behaviors and that you'll have to intervene until they can learn not to do the behavior. You want to do this in ways that are matter-of-fact and not shaming.

Intelligence

As their fine motor skills develop, so does their ability to manipulate and maneuver toys. You will start to see them experimenting with their toys in new ways. They may make their trains go down the tracks or feed their baby doll. They can follow one-step instructions like "Sit down." They might choose to not follow instructions, but *they can*.

WELLNESS

When it comes to the wellness of 18-month-olds, the focus is still on emotional well-being, safety, nutrition, play, sleep, and secure attachments. At this time, there are certain areas of importance that begin to become particularly evident.

* The child is very curious, and their motor skills are stronger than ever. They also have little impulse control, so **safety** is a unique challenge that deserves particular attention.
* Your child's personality is becoming more and more apparent every day. **Recognizing your child's unique temperament** is one of the most valuable elements of parental attunement and learning. It may sound surprising, but being intentional about *knowing* your child can save you (and them) a lot of trouble.

In this section, I felt that it was time to become more intentional about creating a home that is hospitable to the child's needs, differences, and variable emotions while also maintaining a safe environment. Wellness at 18 months is all about keeping the child safe, adapting to their bursting personality, and helping them feel seen. Hopefully, you are also continuing to introduce new foods and being intentional about your child's nutritional and sleep demands. At 18 months of age, food, sleep, play, and parental attention are still the reigning monarchs of child health and well-being.

SAFETY

Your child has a fundamental need for physical protection. Physical protection essentially has three components:

1. *Nurturance*—the degree to which the caregiver is available and consistently able to respond to the needs of their child
2. *Stability*—the degree of predictability and consistency
3. *Safety*—the extent to which the child is free from fear and secure from physical or psychological harm

All three of these components are essential to your child's current and future well-being. If you are struggling in any of these areas, it is imperative that you recruit help. I talk a great deal in this book about the skills of consistent responding (*nurturance*), and the benefits of a predictable home (*stability*) are not particularly hard to imagine. *Safety*, however, can be difficult to achieve for parents because some of the things that make and keep young toddlers safe aren't the things that adults might expect. Let's review those quickly here. Hopefully, you'll get to the bottom of the checklist with a sense of accomplishment because you have been able to achieve each of these items.

Check off each of the following when you are certain that you are meeting your child's safety needs in each area.

☐ A young toddler should never be left alone in the house.

☐ Young toddlers should have regular meals, a safe place to sleep, and several safe adults in their life.

☐ Children should never witness violence or aggression, especially aggression toward their primary caregiver.

NOTE: When a child witnesses aggression toward their primary caregiver, it is considered a toxic stress, meaning that it will affect their brain architecture. If it happens enough, you will actually be able to see this particular kind of trauma on brain scans. Witnessing familial violence is *very serious*.

☐ Do not smoke cigarettes near infants and young toddlers. It causes respiratory problems and has been linked to Sudden Infant Death Syndrome.

☐ Children should be buckled in a rear-facing car seat in the backseat of the car.

☐ Children should never be left alone in the bathtub. All pools should be locked and/or covered. Consider installing an alarm that detects when something (or someone) has fallen in the pool. Never allow yourself to become distracted when near a pool with a young toddler.

☐ Children should never be left in a car alone. Determine a safety protocol so that you have to check the backseat of your car every time you exit the car (maybe put your purse or wallet in the backseat).

☐ Be careful to never expose your young toddler to the ongoing care of someone with a substance abuse problem or major addiction.

☐ All your doors should have child locks, all cleaning chemicals should be kept up and out of reach, all medicines should be kept in cabinets that are up and out of reach, and all electrical outlets should be secured.

TEMPERAMENT RECOGNITION

Working against a child's temperament is frustrating for all parties. When parents don't understand the genetic elements of a child's personality, they are more likely to take a child's inborn characteristics personally, use shame as a discipline tactic, and stunt the child's self-understanding and self-esteem. On the other hand, working *alongside* a child's inborn personality traits eases friction in the relationship, helps the child develop effective coping mechanisms, and decreases parental shame and overcompensation.

A child is born with five largely predetermined (genetic) personality traits. Your child's place on the continuum of each trait will determine their temperament. There is no good place or bad place on the continuum. Each trait is value-neutral, with unique strengths and weaknesses.

1. Intensity of reaction
2. Frustration tolerance
3. Activity level
4. Coping with change
5. Reactions to new people

On each of the following five continuums, place a circle where you believe *your traits and personality* lie, and place a star where you believe *your toddler's traits and personality* seem to lie.

INTENSITY OF REACTION

Some kids go big or go home with their reactions. Get used to it. Some adults are very dramatic, demonstrative, or get easily agitated. Admit it.

CALM PROCESSOR   BIG REACTOR

FRUSTRATION TOLERANCE

Some kids get frustrated and give up easily when faced with a new or difficult task. Others have patience and will stick with a challenge.

I AM TIRED
OF THIS

I HAVE TO CRACK
THIS CODE

ACTIVITY LEVEL

Do you take the world in by sitting and watching or by touching, exploring, and moving? What about your toddler? Some of us learn through still observation; others learn with active movement.

COOL OBSERVER

MOVER AND SHAKER

COPING WITH CHANGE

Some children have a difficult time with changes such as a new babysitter or a deviation in routine. Others go with the flow. Adults are the same way.

GO WITH
THE FLOW

STICK WITH
THE PLAN

REACTIONS TO NEW PEOPLE

How comfortable are you and your toddler with new people and novel situations?

GIVE ME THE
PEOPLE I KNOW

SHOW ME NEW
PEOPLE AND PLACES

RESPONDING TO TEMPERAMENT

Temperament is biologically based, is usually consistent over time, and isn't something that the child chooses or creates. Temperament shapes a child in several meaningful ways. Recognizing the limits, vulnerabilities, and behaviors of their temperament is important for healthy development.

Imagine for a second that your child has a difficult time with change. Because you desire to recognize and respect their needs, it is good for you to accept that school drop-off or transitioning classrooms might be hard for them.

What might be an appropriate way to express temperament recognition and acceptance in this situation?

_____

_____

_____

If you thought that *creating a particularly comforting goodbye routine* would be smart or decided that you wanted to *work closely with their caregiver to help during transitions*, then you are on the right track. Avoidance isn't the answer.

In this scenario, you want to give your toddler the boldness, wisdom, and skills to continue to try new things by providing your extra support and your own creative problem solving in difficult moments. You want to notice your child's challenges and provide buttresses for continued growth that take these challenges into account.

Let's consider each of the five big personality traits that make up a child's temperament. As you consider their day and your values, imagine a scenario in which the child's predilections could create a challenge.

INTENSITY OF REACTION

How might their big reactions or very muted reactions cause difficulty in the future (or currently)?

_____

_____

How can you provide support?

_____

_____

FRUSTRATION TOLERANCE

How might your child's difficulty persisting at challenges or their inability to move on when appropriate cause difficulty in the future (or currently)?

_____

_____

How can you provide support?

_____

_____

ACTIVITY LEVEL

How might your child's sedentary lifestyle or their constant moving and touching cause difficulty in the future (or currently)?

_____

_____

How can you provide support?

_____

_____

COPING WITH CHANGE

How might your child's ability or inability to cope with change and transitions cause difficulty in the future (or currently)?

_____

_____

How can you provide support?

_____

_____

REACTIONS TO NEW PEOPLE

How might your child's slowness or quickness to warm to novel people and situations cause difficulty in the future (or currently)?

_____

_____

How can you provide support?

_____

_____

CRISIS RESOURCES

The best way to get help is with one small step at a time. The first step almost always feels the hardest, but it can usually be done very quickly with one courageous act: Simply say (or type) "I need help." Say these simple words to a trusted someone and let the rest follow. This may mean walking into a random church and saying out loud, "Someone please help me," or making a lunch date with your mother. ASK FOR HELP.

Good parents make mistakes. Great parents get the help when they need it.

National Child Abuse Hotline	1-800- 4A-CHILD
National Domestic Violence Hotline	1-800-799-SAFE
National Parents Helpline	1-855-4A-PARENT
National Alliance on Mental Illness	1-800-950-NAMI
National Suicide Prevention Lifeline	1-800-273-TALK
National Alcoholism and Substance Abuse Hotline	1-800-784-6776
Child Sexual Abuse	1-866-FOR-LIGHT
Human Trafficking	1-888-373-7888

LEARNING

Your young toddler is ready to learn and make sense of their world. Your job is to give them a strong foundation in language and literacy, social-emotional skills, and problem-solving skills so they can consolidate their learning and be ready for the school environment. The very clear truth about toddler learning is that *all this acquisition and consolidation of life* must happen in the context of a responsive relationship with respect, repetition, and routine.

In this section, we will review a few things that you can work on to build your child's thinking and problem-solving skills. We will also review the very best ways that you can begin to build the social-emotional competence necessary for lifelong health, learning, and true school readiness. Social-emotional competencies include self-esteem, patience, persistence, conflict resolution, empathy, staying focused, self-confidence, self-efficacy.

BUILDING THINKING SKILLS

Here is a quick checklist of activities and habits of engagement that strengthen toddlers' thinking skills. Habits of engagement are behaviors that you bring to daily activities with your children that when practiced regularly will shape them in profound ways through relationship, which is how toddlers learn best.

Answer the questions following each item. Feel free to make notes or observations in the margins to build upon all this simple checklist has to offer. These activities are more powerful than you think!

☐ **Allow for lots of repetition**

Repetition strengthens the connections in the brain. What might seem mundane and exhaustingly boring to you is important work for them. Let it happen!

What is some activity, word, or movement that you have noticed your child repeating?

_____

☐ **Provide challenges**

Observe what skills your child has acquired or has almost mastered and then find a new way to push them to work a little differently with that skill. For instance, if they are stacking blocks easily, see if they can be encouraged to build a house with them.

Think about a motor skill or problem-solving task that your child is working on. How can you push them to work differently or challenge them?

_____

_____

☐ **Let your child be a problem solver**

Think of yourself as a *coach*, not as a savior. Wonder out loud how they might accomplish the goal or try new things. You can make suggestions but let them brainstorm solutions, try, and fail. Watch closely for that frustration threshold and be careful not to rescue them before they need it.

Speaking of frustration threshold, how can you tell your child is working hard and beginning to feel aggravated but is not yet ready for intervention? That fine line exists, and you should know where it is.

_____

_____

☐ **Create teachable moments**

Use a daily walk to observe and name colors, shapes, and letters. Use bath time to learn about filling, emptying, sinking, and floating. Label household items, encourage sounds, and observe textures together. The world is your oyster.

Think about your routines or your passions . . . or even just the things your child notices. What are some teachable habits you can begin to incorporate into your interactions?

_____

_____

_____

☐ **Don't be so sure**

If your child uses one object, like a cup, for another purpose, like stacking (rather than drinking) or if they try to roll a cube, let them try. They are trying to understand the laws of the universe through play, and play is the best way. Your corrections and interventions aren't always helpful, so be careful.

What is it like for you to watch your child attempt impossible things or to learn by trial and error? Some parents really struggle with this valuable learning technique.

_____

_____

☐ **You're not the director**

Pretend play is powerful. Ask questions about what you should do or what they would like you to cook, for instance. Ask them what is on the pretend plate at teatime. Don't make assumptions and fill in the gaps. Ask questions and be curious about the story they are trying to tell.

What is it like for you to let your child create the play? Is it boring, exciting, preposterous, confusing, silly? All that is normal. Go with it. Learn the dance of offering suggestions but letting them lead.

_____

_____

BUILDING SOCIAL-EMOTIONAL COMPETENCIES

We discussed that learning in toddlers can be divided essentially into three major categories: language, thinking, and social-emotional. In the previous exercises, we reviewed the parental competencies and activities that support literacy, thinking and problem solving, and language.

Let's walk through some activities and attitudes that build social and emotional competence together.

1. **Create an environment in which children feel safe to express their emotions.** This can be done in a number of ways, but even something as simple as reading a book together or noticing and stating your child's emotions without judgment makes a difference.

What is one small way that you can make sure your home is a safe place to express emotions, big or small, without judgment?

_____

_____

_____

2. **Remember the importance of being emotionally responsive to your child and modeling empathy.**

Imagine that your 19-month-old excitedly starts pulling things off a high table, some of which are breakable. What is an emotionally responsive way to acknowledge their pride (in reaching, making noise, being strong, etc.) yet prohibit this unsafe and unkind behavior?

_____

_____

When your child begins to cry because they want to keep doing the prohibited activity, what is a way to respond with empathy while maintaining the boundary?

_____

_____

Clear expectations and limits are very important to self-esteem and self-efficacy. Do you feel as though your previous responses express clear expectations and limits?

_____

Choose a value to express in the preceding scenario (for example, "We can't throw Mama's special things.") and include it in your response. Make sure that your response now is clear and kind and connects your "no" to your expectations for them.

_____

_____

3. **Keep emotions and actions separate.** An example of this would be the statement "It is okay to be angry, but we don't hit people when we are angry."

Imagine that your child feels very frustrated by their peas (peas are fun for fine motor practice until they aren't) and throws their plate on the ground. How might you acknowledge their feelings while making sure the action is addressed?

_____

_____

4. **Encourage and reinforce socials skills, such as greeting others and taking turns.**

Say your child is "slow to warm" with people, and yet greeting treasured adults, like grandma, is a valued family manner. If your child hides in your chest after you've said, "Let's make sure we smile or wave at Grandma," what is the best course of action?

A. Immediately force them to say hello
B. Model an appropriate greeting and then celebrate when, several minutes later, your child exhibits a prosocial response such as smiling

The correct answer is B. It is gentle and encourages the desired behavior without adding more anxiety. Later, you might practice introductions or greeting scenarios in play or in an otherwise "safe," low-stress situation (like with their favorite babysitter).

5. **Create opportunities for children to solve problems.** This is a great way to build the social-emotional skills necessary for school readiness. You can manage your child's frustrations in a safe space and encourage their creative thinking. If your child is pulling things off the table, you might say, "What can we throw instead?"

Given all that we have discussed, imagine that your child has hit another child. Both toddlers are 20 months old, and you know that hitting is normal and that self-control has not yet developed. How might you respond empathetically, establish clear limits, keep actions separate from feelings, and offer an opportunity to problem-solve?

_____

_____

_____

BOUNDARIES AND ROUTINES

If you haven't started already, now is certainly the time to begin shaping the behavioral routines and patterns that will influence the long-term health of your child. Behavioral routines are simply those routines that are so regular and so consistent that they become habitual and influential for the rest of the child's life. These behaviors fall under a wide variety of domains:

* Toothbrushing
* Television viewing
* Physical activity
* Risk-taking behaviors
* Eating habits

Now is the time to become watchful and intentional about the way these activities become influential routines. A great example is the type, amount, and frequency of foods offered to your toddler. Together, these behaviors affect the child's taste and texture preferences as well as their dietary likes and dislikes. Early learning in this area, coupled with the habits they form regarding routine levels of activity, will affect their risk of obesity.

In this section, you will have the opportunity to become more intentional about your child's behavioral routines. This section will also help you think through your broad expectations and become more intentional about your boundaries. If you didn't read A Note about Keeping Broad Boundaries and Expectations (page 59), go back and do so. Those truths still apply to children at this stage.

IMPORTANT BEHAVIORAL ROUTINES

Your goal with this exercise is to become more intentional about teaching health-promoting behaviors. For each category, I want you to think about the following questions and make notes. Work on creating a sturdy intention that will set your child up for success.

1. What kind of behaviors do you model in this domain?
2. What are the child's needs and limitations?
3. How can you ensure that their habits in this area are health-promoting?
4. Be as practical as possible. Try to paint a picture of how you will support each domain in your daily life.

TOOTHBRUSHING

Children should be brushing their teeth twice a day. Many families find that it is easiest to incorporate this habit into the getting dressed and going to sleep routines.

Consider the four earlier questions and make your answers practical. How can you support this domain in your child's daily life?

_____

_____

_____

_____

TELEVISION VIEWING

Children this age should have zero to very little screen exposure.

Consider the four earlier questions and make your answers practical. If you are using television, how can you limit its use and ensure that the programs your child is viewing are health-promoting? How can you model healthy habits?

_____

_____

_____

_____

PHYSICAL ACTIVITY

Your young toddler needs daily, regular levels of physical activity. They need to move, play, run, walk, and get encouragement to stay active. This isn't exercise; this is the way your family engages in regular activity.

Consider the four earlier questions and make your answers practical. How can you encourage your child to stay active?

_____

_____

_____

_____

RISK-TAKING BEHAVIORS

We need to be careful about the way our young toddlers engage in risk-taking behaviors, like running away from us, refusing to hold a hand in parking lots, climbing to unsafe heights, and so forth. Risk-taking is developmentally appropriate, but we need to watch and shape their impulses while keeping them safe. We should acknowledge their desires to take risks and their frustrations while helping them stay within healthy parameters.

Consider the four earlier questions and make your answers practical. How can you help your child engage in safe risk-taking?

_____

_____

_____

_____

EATING HABITS

Your young toddler needs exposure to a variety of textures and tastes. They should be offered food at times when eating is appropriate. You should begin to get rid of grazing behaviors, and you should begin to monitor distracted eating. Their metabolism and cravings will take shape as you guide their daily food schedule.

Consider the four earlier questions and make your answers practical. How can you help your child develop healthy eating habits?

_____

_____

_____

_____

BROAD EXPECTATIONS AND FIRM BOUNDARIES

Let's introduce a few value categories that might help you shape your expectations so you can be more purposeful and consistent when expressing limitations. Boundaries that are anchored in values are excellent for all ages, but especially for young toddlers. Value-specific limitations tend to be broad and decisive yet with necessary flexibility. As your child ages, knowing when to stand your ground and when to let something slide is an important skill. Remembering the values that underpin a particular limitation or expectation helps.

In the following table, you'll find four value categories that promote child health and well-being. Beside each value, I want you to brainstorm age-appropriate boundaries that support it. I've started you off with one example for each category. Try to add two or three more.

Values	Boundaries
Safety	The child must be held in parking lots.
Health and Nutrition	The child should take a nap every day.

Values	Boundaries
Community Participation	No hitting.
Family and Relationships	Picking up after playtime.

Going back to my earlier emphasis on decisive yet flexible value-driven boundaries, please note my example for the Safety value: "The child must be held in parking lots." The most important thing here is that the child remains *safe*.

If I was in an empty parking lot, waiting on a friend, I might feel like I could be flexible here and let the child down to play. If, however, the child wants to walk every time we approach a busy grocery store, then I might stay very consistent about not being allowed to ever be on asphalt without being held. At this age, boundaries are best when they are a mix of values, consistency, and recognition of the child's temperament.

DISCIPLINE

Your child's capacity for self-control is still very, *very* limited. So much of what you are doing at this age should be a constant, supportive shepherding. This is opposed to an understanding of discipline that is strictly punishment-oriented. Your child is a little more self-and-other aware now, which matters, but you should still be disciplining (or discipling) in a way that heavily emphasizes your watchful eye, your hopeful spirit, and your proud expectations. These are the foundations of discipline at 18 to 24 months. Enjoy your child, and let them feel your enjoyment. Work hard on getting to know their temperament, preferences, and abilities while continuing to work on your broad expectations, boundaries, and gentle limits.

For my husband and me, "gentle limits" meant subtle redirection and firm yet understanding boundaries. When my child was behaving in a way that didn't support our values of gentleness, kindness, patience, or honesty or that wasn't safe, I might have said something like, "Hmm. It looks like you want to practice climbing. How wonderful! Let's try it on something safer." Or "Oh, goodness. When you hit me, it hurts. Hitting hurts. I'll have to put you down if you do it again."

In both scenarios, I am not taking their behavior personally or assuming malicious intention. In the first, I am affirming their desire but saying (in not so many words), "It's okay to be active and curious and to climb, but it isn't okay in all settings." In the latter example, I am not shaming them for hitting, which is *normal at this age*, I repeat: *normal.* But I am also disallowing the behavior and introducing a *natural consequence.* This is gentle yet firm.

At this stage and the next, the refrain "I can't let you do this" or "I will have to stop you until you can stop yourself" should ring through your house like an anthem. There isn't shame or anger in these statements. Rather, you are gently introducing a limit by being understanding, kind, but very clear. Gentleness doesn't mean ambiguity or flexibility. These statements help the parent establish firm and decisive limits.

We will discuss natural consequences as we move forward in the book, but now is a great time to begin thinking about the natural and normal consequences of unwelcome behavior as a way to introduce your limits. Consider the following behaviors and their natural consequences: If you continue to hit me, I cannot hold you. If you throw your water on the ground, I will have to help you drink. If you cannot walk safely by my side, I will have to pick you up.

I call these types of limits "consequence couplets." I have chosen these consequence couplets as examples for a couple of reasons:

1. **They do not dwell on the unwelcome behavior.** *Ignoring the behavior is a very important tactic during this stage. With any luck, you will state the consequence couplet only once or twice: "If you hit me, I will put you down." Then you will simply ignore the hitting behavior, executing the consequence, until the target behavior (not hitting while being held) is accomplished. Then you will remove the consequence and praise the target behavior.*
2. **They are firm and decisive.** *The fact that consequence couplets are brief and can be determined well ahead of time makes them sturdy boundaries that the child can quickly learn to respect. They are also so matter-of-fact that they carry no shame.*

Disciplining Normal Behaviors

At this age, a whole plethora of alarming behaviors is *normal*. For many parents, biting and kicking typically top that list. It is best to remember that just because something is *normal* doesn't mean it is *acceptable*. As a reminder, it is *normal* for a dog to get excited when they see their owner. It is not *acceptable* for them to jump all over people as a result of that excitement. This can be harmful and unsafe. Likewise, it is normal for children to become frustrated and hit at this age. But hitting is not acceptable. By holding onto the difference between normalcy and acceptability, we decrease shame but maintain a decisive limit. In our house, some consequence couplets are treated like laws of physics. My attitude tends to be, "I can't help that this is true, but it's true, simple, and unchanging. It just *is*. I know it's hard; I remember not liking it either, but here we are."

As I have been saying all along, staying calm continues to be a boon in the process of carrying out this kind of gentle, directed, consistent discipline. Other normal behaviors that bother parents at this age include clinging, bedtime resistance, food refusal, and throwing. I think that the bonus discipline chapter in the back of the book will be another helpful resource, but for now remember to prioritize connection in these moments. Use your powers to ignore unwanted behaviors, hold firm to a few valued consequence couplets, and *praise target behaviors like sharing, compliance, kindness, and creativity.*

GENTLENESS AND RESPECT

Our children, even our very young toddlers, need our respect. Throughout their daily lives, we want our children to internalize the feeling of "being enough" and of being respected. We also want them to know what it feels like to receive someone's empathy. We want these things in all our discipline because a child must have the experiences firsthand in order to imitate them or offer them to others. Children learn—and this is very important—from not just what we say but *how* we say it and *how* we relate to them.

If you want your child to respect you and your expectations and to learn from your discipline, you must offer them experiences that thoroughly reflect your belief that *they are whole beings with complex internal lives who long to do well.* You must recognize which expectations are developmentally appropriate. You also should operate completely outside of shame. Shame communicates, "You are bad." Guilt communicates, "You are good, but you have done something that is not allowed."

The distinction between normal and acceptable behavior seems simple but can be very challenging for many parents. Avoiding shame tactics is very much about offering empathy for their typical and developmentally appropriate impulses, struggles, and emotions while *also* offering redirection and/or limits. As an adult, I might have guilt for yelling at my child, but I refuse to feel shame for experiencing frustration and anger. When we stay correctly oriented to guilt and shame or normalcy and acceptability, we can let guilt motivate change (parents should not yell at their children). Shame, on the other hand, stagnates change and can even create more of the unwelcome behavior. This is the very same for children. You and your child are sharing in this process. In fact, you are sharing (or have shared) in many of the same processes.

I often think of this Pema Chödrön quote: "Compassion is not a relationship between the wounded and the healed, it is a relationship between equals." For whatever reason, parents do not often offer their compassion when confronting the unwanted or even dangerous behavior of a toddler. It's a missed opportunity, though, because we have all struggled to learn impulse control, kindness, and the management of our temper. We seem to think that eye-level, empathetic compassion creates a kind of equality that diminishes our power or authority. But that could not be further from the truth. *Respect is effective*. Plus, for many of us, "I have been there. You're okay, but this behavior can't continue," is a much more honest approach. It is respectful and gentle, and it teaches empathy by offering empathy.

This section includes another calming technique. Go back and practice the first calming technique—Take Three Deep, Centering Breaths (see page 67)—and then add this one. We need as many techniques for calming in our tool belts as possible, and practice makes these things more available in the heat of the moment.

This section also includes an explorative exercise that might help you visualize your hopes for your child. We will revisit this exercise in upcoming chapters. Your hopes and vision for both your child and the "ideal child" will be helpful guideposts moving forward. When we do the hard work to honestly sketch out our ideals (no matter how impractical), it can help us be more specific about our interventions and more understanding in our approach.

CALMING TECHNIQUE: USE A MANTRA

A quick and effective variation of our deep-breathing exercise from chapter 1 (see page 67) is to add a three-part mantra. On the first exhale, you might say, "Wait." On the second exhale, you can add, "Calm down," and on the third exhale, you can ask yourself to "Be present." Other options might be "I am // here // for you," "Carefully act // with love // and respect," or "I will // notice // their pain."

What mantra will you use during your breathing practice? It can be one of my suggestions or one of your own. Think carefully of your triggers, your beliefs, or what kind of thing you need to hear in hard moments.

Indicate how you will divide this mantra according to your three breaths as I have done in the preceding examples. Remember, it helps to have a word or two for each breath.

_____ // _____ // _____

Now, go ahead and try it. What was it like, adding a mantra to your breathing practice?

_____

_____

Is there a particular moment in your day with your children or caregiving collaborators when this practice might be particularly helpful?

_____

_____

PAINT A WORD PICTURE

At this point, many of our discipline exercises will build on one another. I believe the first step for incorporating all the wonderful, relational capacities we have discussed into your discipline is to paint a detailed word picture.

If you have a co-parent but aren't working through this book together, that is fine. However, I encourage you to bring them in for this exercise. Come together, take your imaginings, and discuss how the word picture that you each created reflects your values, expectations, and limits.

Describe the behavior and moods of an ideal healthy child. Really be descriptive and imagine as much as you can about this child.

What kinds of things do they say? How do they react to change, stress, frustration, and joy?

_____

_____

_____

_____

_____

_____

_____

_____

What values are indicated in the preceding description?

_____

_____

Compare this imaginary child's temperament with your real child. What's different about their behavior?

_____

_____

CHAPTER THREE

2
YEAR-OLDS

Welcome to the terrific twos! Your two-year-old is a wild, curious little bundle of wide-eyed energy who needs your steady love. Admittedly, two-year-olds have earned a reputation for being completely unreasonable and unpredictable, so this chapter takes a turn toward behavior management and outburst prevention. I have survived the "terrible twos," as they call it, twice now. My experiences were fantastic and fun, largely because I understood each child's temperament. I also developed skills to connect quickly for prompt de-escalation and comfort. Enjoyable toddler parenting is possible, and the skill set to make it happen is teachable.

This chapter will walk you through several exercises that teach skills, solidify important values, and broaden your understanding of your two-year-old's needs and development.

My husband and I were careful and constant in our early introduction of boundaries, so that come their second birthdays, our children weren't shocked by reality. They had been practicing how to wait and make choices since before their first birthday. I am excited to review these and many other skills as you head off into the great unknown of this infamous stage.

TWO-YEAR-OLD MILESTONES

Let's quickly review some milestones. If your toddler doesn't fit the general description of the typical accomplishments, you may want to talk to your doctor, or you may want to simply back up in the book and work on the exercises for 18-month-olds. We want to make sure that your child is ready to be cared for in the particular ways that we describe.

Your child's communication has likely exploded. They can be thoughtful, funny, and curious. They are trying on the varying shapes and sizes of independence in a thousand tiny ways every day. Don't be fooled. They are not adults. They do not have the same neurological capacities for logic, temper management, impulse control, and self-soothing that you do. *You are still their primary source of calm, routine, and wisdom.* Don't expect too little, but definitely don't expect too much. Their combustibility is a normal part of their development. Patience is your primary parenting tool right now.

Muscles

This kid moves at a surprising clip, and no obstacle gets in their way. Amiright? At two years old, your child has far better motor control than even a few short months ago. They can climb, run, jump, stand on one foot, and kick you in the shin. Their fine motor skills allow them to manipulate utensils and other small objects, scribble colorful pictures, and hold a cup in one hand. Their confidence and mastery in this area are but a reflection of the proficiency they feel in other areas as well.

Language and Communication

The dramatic increase in language your toddler is exhibiting has allowed them to finally make meaning of other people's conversations, structure sentences with subjects and verbs, and, sometimes hilariously, insert themselves into social relationships and communities. The gap between their expressive and receptive language is beginning to narrow. They are using language to interpret and create meaning and express their internal world. When they can't verbalize things, frustrations abound. The wonder of it all can be startling.

Social and Emotional

As new skills develop, so does the desire to exercise them. Your child's remarkable physical growth and communication prowess can cause conflict between them and their caregivers. They desire autonomy but still need limits to help them feel safe and manage the mass amount of information they take in every second. Their brains are growing quickly, and it is exhausting. Their abilities and skills have really changed, and two-year-olds overgeneralize this growth to all areas. They feel limitless—and the fact that they are not limitless can be a harsh reality for them.

Intelligence

Your child is entering a whole new world of play and imagination. They use their new motor skills to manipulate objects (such as trucks and dolls), tell stories, and make sense of their world. They can imitate the adults around them and mimic their routines. They are learning to interpret other people's emotions and create new ideas. Their thoughts are both practical and symbolic.

WELLNESS

Encouragement is a powerful tool for the development of self-esteem, but the way it is done matters quite a bit. When done well, praise is a powerful cure for hopelessness and failure. When done poorly, it can create feelings of helplessness in the face of challenge and reduce persistence. Since we want our children to be as resilient as possible, it is good to be intentional about the types of praise that we introduce. Praise has two distinct variations, each of which has very different long-term implications. I want to help you build your skills in *process praise*.

Proper nutrition and good sleep hygiene are still incredibly important for your child. There are plenty of resources, online and from your pediatrician, to help you determine the proper parameters for these things. In this section, we will focus on social-emotional wellness by building your skills of encouragement and praise.

PRODUCT PRAISE VERSUS PROCESS PRAISE

Let's dig into two very different, very powerful styles of praise so that you can see why *the kind of encouragement* you give really matters to the child's developing sense of self and resiliency.

The goal is to positively affect your child's ability to be persistent, tenacious, and less vulnerable to judgment. I will walk you through the differences between the two types of praise, and then I will ask you to write in several examples of process praise that you can use in the future.

Product praise focuses on the child's *performance outcomes*. This sounds like "Great job out there. You scored two goals!" or "You aced the test—I love it!"

Process praise focuses on the child's *efforts and strategies*. This sounds like "I loved watching you play. You ran hard and showed real leadership!" or "I love this picture because you tried something new and you were super creative."

Your child brings you a coloring sheet, filled in everywhere with tons of different colors. You can tell they really tried hard. What is a way to offer process-oriented praise to this wonderful gift?

Product praise negatively affects a child's resilience and makes their self-esteem vulnerable to a poor performance or an undesired outcome.

Process praise positively affects a child's resilience by giving them internalized values that they can use to solve problems.

What are some of the efforts and strategies that you value or that you believe will help your child succeed? Examples include creativity, leadership, hard work, and bravery. Write them on the lines. These are things you can watch for and find opportunities to praise.

Product praise produces a helpless orientation. "When failure strikes, I might as well give up because I can't control who I am."

Process praise produces a mastery orientation. "When failure strikes, I can be persistent because I have control over my effort."

Considering the efforts, strategies, and character traits you identified, what three different simple sentences of encouragement or praise can you use? Make sure your praise focuses on the child's internal locus of control and character while highlighting one of the attributes.

PRACTICING PRAISE

Revisit the strategies, efforts, and values that you believe will help your child succeed (see your work in the previous section).

Choose four of them, and in the far left column, write one in each of the four rows.

In the middle column, I want you to imagine a setting or activity where you might notice this praise-worthy value in your child. Consider coloring, trying to kick a ball, or when they are getting dressed.

In the far right column, write out an example of a *process-oriented praise* that could be used to affirm that particular value.

Value	Setting or activity	Process-oriented praise

LEARNING

This is a year full of wonderful leaps and bounds in development. Your toddler is experiencing drastic growth in their expressive language, their imagination, and their abilities to problem-solve and build relationships. Learning at this stage requires patience. Two-year-olds need calm and present caregivers to help them name and manage their growing internal world of feelings, thoughts, and impulses.

Reading together with your toddler at any age is always a good choice. At two years old, it's transformative. Reading together at this age builds language and vocabulary, creates meaningful conversations, nurtures their critical thinking, and supports their powers of problem solving, attention, and determination. It also provides moments for warm, nurturing touch. When you read with a toddler, you create opportunities outside meltdowns to discuss fantasies, fears, and challenges. You create hospitality toward emotions and demonstrate empathic attunement.

LITERACY: READ THREE TIMES

One way to maximize reading and repetition with a toddler is to be intentional about your goals for each pass through a book. The Rollins Center for Language and Literacy suggests making the first pass about *events*, the second pass about *emotions*, and the third pass about *the story*.

I want you to read each book many more times than three, and I want you to feel free to read it however you and your child like. However, this three-pronged approach is very helpful and will certainly build important skills.

Choose a book that your child loves or one that you're excited to introduce. *Which book are you using?*

THINK-ALOUDS

"Think-alouds" are moments during reading when the parent asks an open-ended question or makes an observation. My favorites are "I wonder why . . ." and "It looks like she is feeling . . . ." I also like to make an observation about the illustrator's choices.

Do you have favorite think-alouds?

_____

_____

FIRST READ: FOCUS ON EVENTS

As you look through the book, write down some think-alouds regarding:

Vocabulary (e.g., "That's a funny word!")

_____

_____

Key events (e.g., "That big, bad wolf is scary!")

_____

_____

The story's beginning, end, or problem

_____

_____

Practice using different tones, voices, and pace to bring the story to life and direct the child's attention.

SECOND READ: FOCUS ON EMOTIONS

Are there emotions in the book? Think about the story, the art, and the characters:
Emotions can be hidden anywhere. Where are they in this book?

_____

_____

What think-alouds can you use to draw the child's attention to the characters'
(or artist's) thoughts and feelings?

_____

_____

As you look through the book, what emotion words might you like to teach? Check
out the Feelings Words box (see page 110) for some good ideas.

_____

_____

THIRD READ: FOCUS ON STORY

What is the story in your book that you may want to explore further with your child?

_____

_____

Ask them to tell you what is happening in the story. The key to think-alouds is for there to be no right or wrong answer. Simply repeat back their answers to them. You're trying to see this story through their eyes. There is no right or wrong way to wonder together.

FEELINGS WORDS

If you work hard to give your kids a robust vocabulary of feeling words and a lot of opportunities to practice expressing their feelings with language, you will save yourself a lot of pain. The big feelings and desires mixed with a limited vocabulary are cause for a lot of meltdowns at this stage.

- Angry
- Bored
- Brave
- Calm
- Cheerful
- Confused
- Curious
- Disappointed
- Embarrassed
- Excited

- Frustrated
- Generous
- Happy
- Ignored
- Impatient
- Interested
- Jealous
- Lonely
- Loving
- Overwhelmed

- Proud
- Sad
- Safe
- Satisfied
- Shy
- Silly
- Stubborn
- Surprised
- Uncomfortable
- Worried

LEARNING SKILLS AT THIS STAGE

Although social-emotional competencies are very important, I also want to provide you with a checklist of skills and activities to practice during your child's second year that will round out their thinking skills and get them school-ready. Although academics aren't necessarily a priority, getting your child ready to succeed in the educational environment matters.

As you go through this list, place a check mark beside the things that you already do regularly. Look back at the end and celebrate what a great job you are already doing!

- ☐ Encourage your toddler to scribble with markers and crayons.
- ☐ Talk with your toddler about their day at dinnertime or bedtime.
- ☐ Regularly plan opportunities for your child to interact with others their age.
- ☐ Encourage your child to use logic by seeing how they make connections. For example, "I am hungry. What should we do next?" or "It is cold outside. I wonder what we should wear?"
- ☐ Use a kitchen timer to help your child learn to wait.
- ☐ Include your child in problem solving whenever possible. "Kevin wants to play with this toy. Is there something else that you can play with or that you might offer him?"
- ☐ Read together.
- ☐ Follow your child's line of vision and notice the things that they are noticing.
- ☐ Ask questions even if they can't answer. Wonder together about cause and effect.
- ☐ Talk with your toddler about things you are doing, especially during food preparation, driving, playing, or doing chores.
- ☐ Acknowledge and label feelings while setting limits. "I know this is your favorite toy. Still, we are not allowed to grab it from our friends. I know it is frustrating. How can I help?"
- ☐ Avoid yes or no questions. Instead, be open-ended. "Tell me about . . ." or "What don't you like about . . . ?"

- ☐ Don't be afraid of tantrums. They happen. The less you react, the more quickly they can recover. Count to 10 or practice a calming technique.
- ☐ Label your child's feelings. Validation always has to come before redirection or assistance coping. A child won't accept your wisdom until they feel your care.
- ☐ Use pretend play to help your child handle new or challenging situations. If you ran into a problem yesterday, act it out with dolls today and wonder about better solutions.
- ☐ Let your child lead the play.
- ☐ Encourage your child's problem-solving skills with puzzles.
- ☐ Your toddler is asking questions. Ask them what they think before you answer. Be encouraging.
- ☐ Use big challenging words around your kids. They won't always get them, but new words will create curiosity and conversation.

PLAN TO PRACTICE

Last time I introduced a learning skills checklist, I suggested that you grab a calendar and plan to practice each skill, one day at a time. It seems silly to practice such simple things, but if you make a note about it and try hard at one particular thing each day, you will be surprised at how quickly your parenting skills expand.

Go ahead; mark these skills on this calendar template. Then grab a stack of sticky notes. Write the appropriate skill down on several notes each morning and stick them in several places (car, playmat, kitchen sink) so that you don't forget to practice. *What fires together, wires together.*

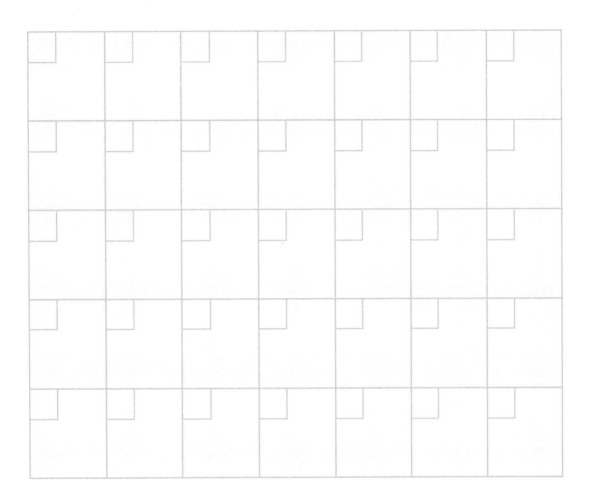

BOUNDARIES AND ROUTINES

As your toddler becomes increasingly aware of their individuality and their growing powers of movement, thought, and language, they are driven to assert themselves. If your child isn't occasionally expressing their likes and dislikes in demanding, angry, or rude ways—then Houston, you have a problem. These things signal healthy neurological growth, happening in the context of a healthy parent–child relationship. Further, their "upstairs brain," as Daniel Seigel and Tina Payne Bryson call it, is at the very beginning stages of development. This means that their capacity for self-control, logic, coping, and waiting is still very small.

In this section, I am going to help you develop four of the crucial parenting skills for children at this age and stage. The literature on toddler parenting suggests many wonderful things, but all agree on these four, and I can attest to their value.

* Staying calm
* Giving choices
* Validating feelings
* Setting limits

Families that know how to stay calm, give choices, validate feelings, and set appropriate limits have the basic skills to intervene when the children are agitated. They can prevent further upset, create a loving environment, and avoid overly frequent explosions of temper.

People often come to me wanting to know what to do when their child has a tantrum. We will cover those things, too, but I always start with *prevention*. "I hear your family is struggling through the tyrannical demands of your toddler, but first, let's see if we can reduce the frequency of outbursts." Not only do these skills curtail the number of tantrums, they also make de-escalation much easier to accomplish.

The exercises in this section focus on three of the four skills. *Staying calm* is also important, but we address that skill in each discipline section at each stage (see pages 21, 66, 94, 123, 148, and 172). Feel free to jump through each chapter to garner support in the very important (and very challenging) skill of "keeping your cool."

GIVING CHOICES

Giving toddlers choices helps them feel like they have power and control, which is great because two-year-olds are power-hungry. They have skills, desires, and a flourishing internal world. They want some control. It's natural.

Are you a planner? Do you feel most comfortable when you're in total control of the details of your day and your child's day?

Yes / No

Many parents believe that if they handle all the details and choices, their toddler's day will be maximally efficient and will run smoothly. That is becoming less and less true as your child ages. The time lost by giving your child a choice is nothing compared with the inefficiency of a power struggle with a two-year-old.

Are there certain routines or activities during which your toddler is beginning to exert control, perhaps by fussing, resisting, refusing, or otherwise having a tantrum?

_____

_____

I wonder: Are these areas over which you are exerting control but could loosen your grip and begin offering choices?

The key to giving children choices is first deciding what choices you will allow them to make and then making those choices clear. In the thinking skills sections, we have been working on asking open-ended questions like "What do you love about the color purple?" **Choices, on the other hand, should *not* be open-ended.**

How can you reframe the following open-ended decisions so that your child has two or three predetermined choices? I've provided an example for each of the first three questions. Try to add two or three more to the ones I've given you and then create some closed-ended choices to replace the last three questions.

What would you like to wear today?	Would you like to wear the red leggings or the blue leggings?
What do you want to do before bedtime tonight?	Which book would you like to read right now?
Do you want to go for a walk?	Would you like to ride in the stroller or be pulled in the wagon during our walk today?
What do you want for lunch?	
Are you ready for bed?	
Let's have art time!	

Open-ended questions encourage a child's imagination, thinking, and language skills, but *open-ended decisions* are overwhelming. Toddlers want power and control, *but not too much of them*. Too much control is upsetting to toddlers and causes tantrums.

As a general rule, the decisions you offer:

* ✴ Should include two or maybe three clear choices
* ✴ Should not affect the structure or timing of routines
* ✴ Should be choices that you can and will be able to honor

Think about a situation in which you and your toddler are having regular struggles. How can you introduce choices into this scenario so that the child might appropriately exert their power?

VALIDATING FEELINGS

Feelings are not the problem. The problem is what your child is doing with their feelings. **Your job is to tune in to your child's experience, have age appropriate expectations, and validate their feelings.** Validating your child's feelings helps them label and make sense of their experience, which in turn helps them to manage their feelings in acceptable ways. At two years old, your child's capacity for self-control is *very* limited. Stay calm, stay present, and validate.

Call to mind a troubled experience that you have had with your toddler in the past few days. What is one recurring frustration that seems to have developed recently?

I will offer my own story as an example to help guide you through this opportunity:

I am married to a farmer. When my daughter was two, harvest season hit her like a ton of bricks. Almost overnight, her father was gone. I noticed the transition as well, but since it was my seventh or eighth season with him, I wasn't attending to his absence in nearly the same way that she was. A couple of behaviors started almost immediately. One, she became obsessed with the rituals and routines of her doll. Feeding her, bathing her, and putting her to bed became a very rigid process that would become explosive if interrupted. It was miserable, but the change was stark enough to get my attention. Two, she started having fits during times of transition. Leaving the house was brutal.

ALL BEHAVIOR HAS MEANING

At this age, children use behavior as frequently as they use language. *You have to consider the context and experience of the child* if you want to intervene effectively or prevent future outbursts.

As a rule, these are the questions I try to ask when trouble hits. Depending on the size and frequency of the problem, I work through them quickly or slowly. You can work through them now using the troubled experience you described earlier.

   1. *What is your child struggling with? Are they tired, hungry, overwhelmed, frustrated, scared, or angry?*

_____

_____

For example, my daughter was suffering a loss. The routines that typically involved her dad were suddenly very different. Things had changed. She didn't have the mental capacity to understand the seasonal lifestyle changes of the farm, and I hadn't considered it enough to remind or reassure her.

2. *What do they need from you to cope with these feelings?*

_____

_____

I had to consider whether my daughter needed simple reassurance or something more. Did she need me to make time for the rigidity of her doll's routines or to respect that she was doing important work in that play? Did she need me to take her to visit her father at work at predictable times?

3. *What do you know about your child's temperament? Are they slow to warm, or do they have difficulty with transitions or exhibit a low frustration tolerance? You may want to revisit the section on temperament recognition (see page 75) for help here.*

_____

_____

My daughter appreciates sameness and routine. She is very loyal and likes a small number of people. She expects those people to tend to her and give her the attention she needs. She doesn't like riding in the car.

EMPATHIZE WITH THEIR FEELINGS

Given what you have answered, what might you say to your child during the heat of the moment? What might you say during an intimate teaching moment when all is calm? Make sure you're labeling and supporting the experience of their emotions.

In a quiet teaching moment, I said something like "Things have really changed. Daddy is gone a lot. I wonder if you miss having him here at dinner and at bedtime. I miss him, too. Would you like it if I took you to have lunch with him?" In the heat of the moment, I said, "It is hard to leave the house when you think Daddy might come home. He won't be home until much, much later, I promise." And then I made more time to accommodate what she thought her "doll" needed. It was truly spectacular the way she used her doll to show me how she wanted to be cared for.

Heat of the moment:

_____

_____

Teaching moment:

_____

_____

ACTION

After I wondered about the meaning of the behavior and validated her feelings, the action I took was decisive and confident. I was kind of guessing (she didn't have the verbal ability to talk to me about her abstract feelings and experiences with the time, the harvest, her father, and her desires). But I felt that I made an informed consideration and acted as empathically as I could, and the behavior abated.

* **Label the feeling.** "You feel sad and scared that you might miss him or that he won't come back."
* **Anticipate the behavior.** I know that routines make my daughter feel safe and that leaving the house will be difficult as long as she has fears about her father returning when we aren't home.
* **Communicate your confidence.** "This is hard, isn't it? You can get through it, and I am here to help."
* **Don't take the bait.** If your child is being really mean and grumpy, don't let it affect you. Comfort them and validate their feelings when the timing is right. Address the feeling, not the behavior.

What action can you take, if any, to prevent further outbursts? Are there changes you can make or ways that you can account for your two-year-old's temperament?

SET FIRM LIMITS

Self-regulation takes years to develop. Consequently, children really need your regulation in their lives. They don't have the capacity for much forethought, impulse control, logic, or perceptual reasoning, so they need a reliable frontal lobe (*yours!*) in their life to provide common sense and guidance.

Quick Tips

* ✳ Don't end statements like "It is time to go" with a question mark. Don't make the mistake of saying, "Are you ready to go?" Be decisive. Make sure the limit is what you want before you set it.
* ✳ When children don't like a limit such as "You can't eat this candy," empathize with that frustration but stand firm. You can be firm without being angry.
* ✳ When they are very upset, don't take it personally. Ignore behavior that is meant to express a feeling. Respond to the feeling, not the behavior.
* ✳ Collaborate with your caregivers. Make sure everyone is expressing and holding the same limits so that your child doesn't feel so confused that they test your limits.

Remember, your child isn't capable of necessarily imagining and instituting these limits themselves, so it is time that you sat down and really thought about what limits you might want to introduce to your child.

Here are four helpful prompts for guidance:

1. What kind of values do you want to teach or build?
2. What kind of person do you want your child to become?
3. What kind of community participant you would like them to be?
4. Consider the values of their other caregiving environments. What attitudes should their behavior affirm to avoid trouble or shame in those environments?

Here are some of the limits and expectations I had for my children when they were two years old: saying hello and goodbye, waiting, not running in the house, not jumping on furniture, not tearing our books, writing or scribbling only where appropriate, no hitting, and matching the volume of their voice to their setting.

Did I expect them to be able to do these things well? *No.* But did I hold these expectations firm, gently guide the child, and remind them until they got it? *Yes.*

What are the limits that you can set in place that will help create safe action and sensible behavior from your child? What values are you building?

DISCIPLINE

I know you're eager to dive into discipline. Your child can feel like a tyrannical jerk sometimes, and *you want action*. I get it. But believe it or not, this whole chapter has been, on some level, about discipline. For toddlers, the skills that we have reviewed are the foundation for all effective discipline.

* Understanding their limits
* Holding your limits
* Expressing empathy and offering validation
* Thoughtfully considering their behavior and trying to create solutions that teach, comfort, and prevent further escalation

Luckily, we have been working on these things all chapter. In addition to these, your *discipline* at this age, which is to say your *caring behavior management and teaching,* should also include an ample dose of two additional things:

* Ignoring inconsequential, unwelcome behaviors
* Selectively praising all nonproblematic, value-affirming behaviors

In chapter 6, we will dive deeper into the differences between consequential and inconsequential behaviors as well as ways to redirect problematic behavior toward value-affirming behaviors. But in this chapter you have already reviewed so many of the important elements of effective praise, empathy, and limits. Great work.

I want to leave you with one more gentle reminder:

You are the anchor in the storm. You are a teacher. You can offer natural consequences . . . but be prepared to comfort their big emotions. Your first job is as comforter and teacher. Your role is not punishment. **Discipline is not punishment, and you should never, ever, under any circumstances, spank or hit your child.**

Spanking

Given all that we know about its poor results and its long-term negative effects, corporal punishment is no longer an acceptable means of behavior management. Spanking is a topic that has spawned an outpouring of research much too great to reference in one volume. But the conclusions are unequivocal: *Uses of force like yelling and spanking do not work.*

To this, parents will tell me, "It worked for me" or "It works for my kids." To that argument, all I can say is, "No, it doesn't." Parents appreciate the short-term effect. They feel it was an effective method in their childhood only because more effective methods weren't employed or experienced. *Fear can work on some children, but it is never as effective as hope and love.*

I can assure you, because I have culled through almost every academic journal on the subject, that if spanking felt like an effective tactic to you as a child, then you are *by far* the exception. The majority of children experience a worsening of behavior, an uptick in aggressive acting out, lasting resentment, and confusion. Science should move us forward. We used to think cigarettes were a benign habit and cribs could be painted with lead. Now we know better. Let this same force for advancement change the way we view corporal uses of force. The research is decisive: *Using force is harmful.*

CALMING TECHNIQUE: REVIEW OF SYSTEMS

1. Stop where you are and draw your attention to your body. You may want to close your eyes. Keep your hands by your side
2. Notice the back of your head and neck. Notice the way your head rests on your neck. Try to relax through these small muscles so that your head feels delicately balanced on top of your neck.
3. Notice your shoulders. Bring them to your ears with tension, and then relax them.
4. Notice your elbows, forearms, and hands.

5. Feel the tension in your forehead, in your jaw, or in your throat. Relax.
6. Notice the way the chair is holding your body or the way the ground is strong beneath your feet.
7. Notice your legs. Wiggle your toes and relax through your thighs and knees.

If relaxing any of these major muscle groups is difficult, try tensing the muscles very tightly, counting to five, and then releasing. Make sure that when you release, you notice the way the relaxation feels. It is very different from the tension.

How was this experience?

_____

_____

You might begin by practicing this during a routine. I also think this review of systems is very powerful if you try it during different emotional states. *What do you notice about your body when you are:*

angry?

excited?

content or relaxed?

CHAPTER FOUR

3
YEAR-OLDS

Just when you thought the "terrible twos" were coming to an end, and with that a cessation of your child's moodiness, you start hearing people use the word "threenager." I'm not sure why people feel compelled to create such unhelpful labels. I assume it's the same compulsion that leads news anchors to call a winter storm "snowmageddon" or "snowpocalypse," as if the fate of Earth rests on how quickly one Rhode Islander can shovel his sidewalk.

The sad truth is that our brains are biologically predetermined to focus on the bad and diminish the importance and frequency of the good. So, when your neighbor delivers a pile of exaggerated stories about their terrible two-year-old or their rebellious three-year-old, remember that parenting a three-year-old is much, *much* more fun than anyone will ever say.

Three-year-olds are fun and curious. They do have particularly strong opinions, but if you listen closely and continue to be interested, you'll find that these opinions reflect a blossoming personality. They are eager and loving. Their developing thinking skills are endlessly amusing. After their teeth have been brushed, the stories have been read, and the lights are off, lie down with your child. People don't often mention it, but pillow talk with a three-year-old is one of life's greatest pleasures.

I want to set you up for a successful year of joy, laughter, connection, and growth.

THREE-YEAR-OLD MILESTONES

Milestone achievements are still happening, but largely, everything is much less obvious and more gradual now than with a younger toddler. Even though their skills have always been building on one another, now things really feel much more cumulative.

You'll start to hear friends who don't see the child very often say, "I can't believe how much they have changed," but for you, these revelatory moments are less common. The three-year-old child is spectacular, and their skills will surprise and impress you, but nothing feels quite as profound as those big early milestones. It is hard to miss your toddler's walking milestone. Now, those same kinds of joyful moments require intimacy and often happen during sweet moments of responsivity and tender interaction or when you least expect it.

Muscles

Your child is running, jumping, climbing stairs, and surprising you with their agility. Proclivities for certain activities are beginning to develop, and it is a pleasure to watch. Is your child clumsy, coordinated, artistic and measured, wild and loose, musical, or athletic? Soon you'll know. Enjoy!

Language and Communication

Talking with your three-year-old is starting to be a lot of fun. They can carry on conversations a few sentences at a time. They can speak to and be understood by other people, which can be hilarious and surprising. They can ask fully formed questions and follow instructions with more than one step. They can name friends and speak about their experiences. They have words for most things in their familiar environment.

Social and Emotional

Even though they aren't yet able to share or cooperate with the play agenda of others (if they can, this is rare), they do have a broader array of prosocial behaviors. Their play is interactive, they have empathy, and they will comfort others who are hurt and crying. They can play games and understand the impact of their behavior. Their behavior has a lot of meaning, and their understanding of rules is beginning to take shape. Parents can begin to expect more mature behavior and even surprising manipulations or hidden intentions. Their understanding of other people's cues and expectations grows every day.

Intelligence

Wow. Over the next year you will see an explosion of imagination. The largest change will be the incorporation of fantasy. Now your child can create circumstances and ideas that are outside their own experience, which they will use to play through difficult or confusing situations. They will also develop fears and even phobias. When fantasy bursts onto the scene, parents begin to notice just how blurry the line between their children's imagination and sense of reality can be at first. Nights may be more difficult for a while because of this.

Their problem-solving skills continue to improve and now extend to puzzles and more complex three-dimensional tasks like building. Reading is more cooperative, and the child's growing understanding of symbols will begin to make them curious about written words.

WELLNESS

Parenting a three-year-old is wonderful but can be difficult. Ruptures in the relationship, which happen often, typically occur when a parent fails to meet the emotional needs of the child by overreacting, underreacting, or mis-attuning. Children can also be the source of rupture as they too overreact, withdraw, and struggle to manage their impulses, desires, and anger. These types of "failures" likely feel much more frequent now. At this stage, many parents even report feeling shame or hopelessness over their parent–child dynamic.

Ruptures are simply a break in the nurturing connection between a parent and child. They are inevitable and common and can be transformed into something helpful with just a little thought and skill. We call this the *rupture and repair process*, and fortunately there is no need for shame or hopelessness. The rupture and repair process is powerful, and when done well it builds resilience, thoughtfulness, and empathy; it deepens your relationship and creates trust.

Family Relations published a study in 2010 that determined these early reparative interactions provide a foundation for the development of the child's emotional and behavioral regulation skills. Many other studies before and since have contributed to this same conclusion. The goal of good parenting at this stage isn't *perfection*, it's *persistence*.

The key to creating a sense of consistency, connection, and security in any parent–child relationship (a cornerstone to lifelong wellness) is not the absence of ruptures and perfect attunement but rather the parent's persistent "moving toward" (that is to say, returning to connection) after rupture. "Moving toward" and repairing is a great competency to develop as we begin to introduce more disciplinary and positive parenting techniques.

In an effort to stem the tide of shame and helplessness that happens during this brief stage, the focus of our Wellness section (page 159) will be building resilience in your child and in your relationship.

INTERACTION DEBRIEFING

Slowing down, observing what is happening, and responding with care can easily become a habit. We call this kind of parenting *responsive parenting*, which is the opposite of *reactive parenting*.

Let's start with a simple four-step debriefing exercise that you can come back to again and again when you are feeling stuck, frustrated, or even successful. Think:

* Recall
* Reflect
* Reconnect
* Respond

These things will help you be thoughtful and introduce purposeful actions, which will be more successful and lead to more connection.

RECALL

Bring a difficult moment to mind. It can be a common struggle or a major battle, but try to recall a specific instance. Write about the moments that preceded the incident as well as the incident itself.

_____

_____

REFLECT

How did you feel?

_____

_____

What was your first reaction?

_____

_____

Why do you think you reacted that way?

_____

_____

RECONNECT

Think about your child's behavior cues and verbal or facial expressions.

What do you think your child was feeling or needing?

_____

_____

What was going on before that moment?

_____

_____

What did your child learn from the interaction?

_____

_____

RESPOND

What kind of outcome did you want from this situation?

_____

_____

How could you have taken the context and your child's temperament into account at the time?

_____

_____

10 HABITS FOR HEALTHY RUPTURE AND REPAIR

I have provided the following checklist of 19 action steps, divided by the 10 core competencies of resilient parent–child relationships. If you can begin to incorporate just one of these habits into your daily parenting practice, it will change the outcomes of your repair and reconnection attempts in no time. This may seem like a lot, but is there anything more important than making sure your relationship with your child is nurturing and resilient? This stuff matters!

Remember: Your child is three now. Their ability to protest, withdraw, and be hurtful can feel bigger than ever. You can be hurtful, too. It is a frustrating time. Rather than feel shame, let's work on reconnecting, preventing future instances, and building trust.

1. Eat some humble pie

Most adults report that they had very few satisfying moments of reconciliation or amends with their parents when they were children. I once sat in a room of adults who were asked, "How many have ever received an apology from their parents?" Less than a third of them raised their hands. Yet, when the same group of adults were asked if they could recall instances where an apology was warranted, almost every person had a hand in the air.

This absence of recognition, confession, and reconciliation is confusing and hurtful to children, especially when the parent behaves in a way that is otherwise prohibited (yelling, spanking, lying). As parents, we should seek honest reconciliation that willingly admits wrong, if necessary.

- ☐ Ask for forgiveness. *State what you did wrong, how you wish you had done it differently, and use the words, "Will you forgive me?"*
- ☐ Grant forgiveness. *When they apologize, say the words "I forgive you," and offer a warm hug.*

2. Pause and connect

Give yourself a moment to breathe. If you have a history of trauma, your brain might need several moments to get back in connection mode and be ready to listen. *Always connect first*, and then your boundaries, discipline, and redirection will be more effective.

- ☐ Drop to your child's eye level and offer a loving touch.
- ☐ Listen and look for the emotions behind your child's behavior. *When you or your child are feeling explosive and dis-regulated, don't try to explain or lecture.*
- ☐ Repeat, repeat, repeat. *When your child expresses their experience of the rupture, repeat back to them what you hear, using a lot of their own words.*

3. Offer empathy

Setting boundaries is *by far* one of the most loving things you can do for your children, especially when they are upset. Unfortunately, boundaries can cause arguments and anger. You can join with them in experiencing your boundary, offering your maturity, experience, and support.

- ☐ Communicate understanding. *Rather than changing the boundary, try saying, "I know this is hard, but I am not going to change my mind. I will be here to comfort you as you deal with this difficult thing."*

4. Find yourself

Are you in reactive mode or receptive mode? *Find yourself on this continuum without judgment.* Is your body tense, or is your face angry? Are your thoughts rushed and repetitive? Or are you open, relaxed, curious, and feeling cooperative?

- ☐ Take time to determine whether you were being reactive or receptive. *Were you modeling listening, gentleness, and curiosity, or were you being defensive, dishonest, and punitive?*

- ☐ Offer an invitation. *If you decide you were being reactive, invite them into your process of trying to be more receptive next time. You might say, "I felt tense in my body and didn't listen. I am going to work hard at taking three deep breaths and counting to 10 when I feel myself getting mad."*

5. Model that everyone makes mistakes

What is the point in your child believing that you have never struggled with emotion regulation or patience? You are still having to work hard on these things. Sharing a bit of your story builds connection and compassion.

- ☐ Reassure them that you love them and that *they are good*, even when *their behavior is bad.*

6. "Feeling felt"

Your child will not be receptive to your efforts at repair unless you model that you are trying to understand their experience, needs, and wants.

- ☐ Ask for clarity.
- ☐ Wonder with them what it felt like to be with you in that moment.
- ☐ Repeat what they heard, felt, or saw. *When your child offers a gross misinterpretation of your words and affect, it can hurt. Do not attempt to clarify or correct until you have made sure they feel understood.*

7. Know your imperfections

Do you know your pet peeves and the things that trigger your temper? Do you know what it feels like to be with you when you are angry or annoyed?

- ☐ Ask a friend or partner about your body language, voice, and tactics when you are mad.
- ☐ Be honest about the cause of your overreaction. *If you overreacted to something your child did in the car because driving makes you anxious, fess up. If your day has been garbage and you were short with them at dinner, let them know it isn't their fault.*

8. Help your child narrate the day's events

☐ Invite your child to tell the story of their day, incorporating their moments of rupture and repair with their friends and with you.

☐ Find a way to make this storytelling a daily moment.

9. Give your children your time

If you're feeling that your ruptures have been huge, frequent, and consistently unrepaired lately, start over and give them more of your time.

☐ Find a moment to build something together (for example, a Lego set, a block tower, or a sandcastle). *Cooperative play is reparative.*

☐ Don't make them speak if they don't want to. Simply be together in love.

10. Act quickly

Remember that at the heart of rupture is a disconnection between you and your child. When your child is disconnected from you, especially if the feeling is chronic, it negatively affects a lot of areas, and the frustrations build.

☐ Do what you can. *Feeling overwhelmed is inevitable. Once you're calm, reconnect as soon as possible.*

ℓℓ LEARNING ℓℓ

Your child is likely learning new words and phrases every day. The best way to enhance their communication skills and prepare them to read is to talk to them as often as possible! Responsive interactions with a conversational partner are powerful at this age. Most of their learning is still done in relationships and during routines—not during classroom activities. Planning for these activities and thinking of fun ways to introduce new words or even new languages is one of the best parts of this stage. Their ability to think symbolically is also readying them to recognize numbers, letters, and even a few words. Have fun!

PLANNING INTERACTIONS FOR LANGUAGE GROWTH

The following table will remind you of some of the most fertile times to interact with your child with authenticity, with fun, and with lots of conversation. Planning for conversational interactions can have surprising results. You may notice that you're more attentive and present and that your child's vocabulary expands quickly. I encourage you to make each of these moments *phone free* as well. Your child deserves moments when they can expect your undivided attention.

Remember that true school readiness is about so much more than academic skills. It is their conversation and relationship skills coupled with emotional competencies that will give them the greatest leg-up and ensure a successful start.

Here I have listed several moments in your day that tend to be flush with opportunities for conversation. I have also offered tips that might help those moments be more fruitful. In the third column, plan a few vocabulary words that you would like to include. The fourth column provides room for you to make notes, if necessary, after considering the following questions:

1. What do I know about my child that will help me be optimally responsive to them?
2. How will I use what I know about my child's temperament, preferences, or abilities to be more responsive?
3. How will I engage in more responsive interactions during this part of our day?

Opportunities in your schedule	General tips for powerful interactions	New vocabulary or phrases to introduce	Con-siderations
Waking up	Engage in a song; call the child by name; comfort them or offer them a warm touch; tell them what's next; acknowledge how they are feeling	dreams, dazed, happy, grumpy	
Diaper changing/ potty time	Talk about what the child is doing; sing songs or nursery rhymes; tell them what you're doing	diaper, change, toilet, remove, wet, stinky, sing, smile, tickle	
Meals	Honor every attempt to communicate; combine gestures with talk; invite them to prepare food with you; invite them to prepare the table; talk about the ingre-dients; let them taste and smell; sit with the child while they eat; use back-and-forth conversation; sit face-to-face; do not take out your phone	food, spices, microwave, heating, cooling, utensils	

Opportunities in your schedule	General tips for powerful interactions	New vocabulary or phrases to introduce	Con-siderations
Dressing	Give them choices between two or three items; use humor and be silly; invite them to try to dress themselves; watch for appropriate frustrations and inter-vene when necessary; talk about the weather and your activities	weather, pants, skirts, button, zipper, laces, closet	
Reading	Tell them the meaning of key words; encour-age them to point to pictures; read rhymes in a singsong rhythm; talk about the illustra-tions; ask them their thoughts about the colors; point to the illustrations as you say the words	illustrator, artist, author, pages, title	
Getting ready for a nap	Use a calm voice; sing songs; lie beside your child; imagine the dreams they'll have; tell a story from the first part of the day; ask them what makes them comfortable	blanket, sheets, still, pillow	

NEW PROBLEM-SOLVING SKILLS

One of the coolest things that happens around your child's third year is the development of *logic*, or the ability to reason about why things happen. You may notice your child asking, "Why?" until you are both breathless. The best thing about this incessant "why-ing" and the development of logic is that they can now begin to participate in problem solving. Not only can they problem solve, they *should*. Including them in finding solutions to tough problems, especially behavior or disciplinary problems, is very helpful. Life is a series of problems to solve every day, so nurturing this skill in your toddler is one of the greatest gifts you can give them.

PRACTICING PROBLEM SOLVING
IN RELATIONSHIPS

As always, the approach to discipline should include empathy, understanding, curiosity, and connection. But now, we can begin to partner with our child to solve the problem *together*. In other words, you can now start asking them if they can help you think of a solution. You can discover their surprising (and sometimes revelatory) ideas about why the problem keeps happening and how you can stop it together. Practicing their new problem-solving skills is a learning opportunity for both parents and children.

Child's behavior: Refuses to stop doing something that you have asked them to do, such as throw a ball in the house

Parent reminder: It is normal for a child to practice their new motor skills and to be curious about cause and effect. They aren't doing it to annoy you.

How can you validate your child's feelings and explain the rule? (For example, "I know you're excited and eager to throw the ball. I can tell that you're proud of how strong you've become. That's great, but unfortunately we can't practice throwing in the house.")

How can you partner with them to problem-solve? (For example, "What can we do differently when you want to practice throwing? Can you ask to go outside, or should we go together when I finish what I am doing?")

_____

_____

Child's behavior: Won't cooperate with a transition such as stopping play to leave the house and go to day care

Parent reminder: Transitions are hard for young children. Sometimes they need adjustment time and support to cope.

How can you validate your child's feelings and explain the rule?

_____

_____

How can you partner with them to problem-solve?

_____

_____

Child's behavior: Demonstrates aggressive behavior like hitting, kicking, or biting

Parent reminder: Your child isn't a sociopath, and the attacks aren't personal. They are learning to deal with big and angry emotions.

How can you validate your child's feelings and explain the rule?

_____

_____

How can you partner with them to problem-solve?

_____

_____

Child's behavior: Tells a lie to try to get out of trouble, like saying they didn't steal a cookie when you know they did

Parent reminder: Lying is a normal developmental phase. Calling them out on it directly can actually lead to more lying. Go straight to the rule to avoid a power struggle about whether they lied.

How can you validate your child's feelings and explain the rule?

_____

_____

How can you partner with them to problem-solve?

_____

_____

BOUNDARIES AND ROUTINES

Routines continue to be the best way to help your child feel safe, which in turn helps them learn. Plus, routines are still the primary ground for moments of friendship and teaching, and your child expects them. Boundaries also make your child feel safe because they put a limit on the tyranny of their needs and demands (and a toddler's demands *are* tyrannical). Unfortunately, though, these limits and expectations can occasionally cause upset despite their overall benefit. In this section, we will practice using "time-ins," which create a safe space for calming down but keep the parent and child connected. This is opposed to the reckless use of timeouts, which remove the parent's calming presence and momentarily sever the connection between parent and child (see page 26 to review how to properly use a timeout).

We will also review the use of *positive directions* rather than the strict use of prohibition. Children respond better when you ask them *to do* something ("Please sit up straight.") rather than tell them what *not to do* ("Don't slouch."). Using positive directions decreases acting out behaviors and is more appropriate for your child's development at this age.

"TIME-IN" SKILLS

Time-ins are basically just timeouts, but instead of your child being alone, you stay with them to offer comfort and support. There are several skills that can be incorporated to make time-ins feel more comforting, be more effective, and create lasting change. Walk through each of these skills and answer the following questions to become more prepared to make time-ins effective.

1. Create a safe space.

Where can you and your child establish a "cozy corner"?

_____

Write out what you will say to your child about the purpose of the space and its appropriate use.

_____

_____

_____

2. Be realistic about what the time-in will accomplish.

If it isn't realistic for your child to develop remorse or understand why they became upset, what else can you expect?

_____

_____

Are there exercises you can teach your child now (that is, when they aren't upset) that will help them effectively use the time-in to become relaxed or receptive?

_____

_____

Consider the calming techniques you have been practicing: What is the most effective way for you to calm yourself when you and your child have escalated emotions?

_____

_____

3. Choose a time limit.

You can end the break when the child is calm, or you can set a timer. *Which seems best for you?*

_____

If you set a time, what amount of time will you choose? Two minutes? Five minutes?

_____

How can you tell when your child is calm enough to be redirected?

_____

_____

What is a consistently engaging activity that you and your child both enjoy that will help you both continue to calm down while reconnecting?

_____

_____

4. Ignore the behavior, not the child.

Although I don't have a way to prepare you for this, I can offer a gentle reminder: Validate the feeling, communicate that you see the emotion, and then move on. You can continue to restate that you see their struggle, but do this while you are going about life. Once they have calmed down, reconnect in a new activity without addressing the tantrum. Just move on. The tantrum is a communication about needs and emotions; the behavior itself isn't as important as assuring the child that you have seen and heard the pain and that you are willing to help them in the future.

POSITIVE DIRECTIONS

Complete the following table. As you formulate your more appropriate response, consider whether you might also need to first *validate the feeling*. You may have to be creative in your responses, but do your best to imagine this scenario playing out in your life and then simply fill in the blanks. I've provided a couple of examples. Try to add two or three more to the ones I've given you, and then create positive directions for the other prohibitive statements.

The point is to get in the habit of using less prohibitions and more positive directions. Remember: *Positive behavior guidance* tells children what you would like them to do, while punishments and prohibitions only designate the behaviors that you wish they would stop.

Instead of saying:	Guide behavior by saying:
"Quit kicking his blocks over."	"If you want to play with the blocks, please ask. Say, 'Henry, can I play with the blocks now?'"
"Stop running in the house."	"When you're inside, I want you to walk. Running is for outside."
"Don't throw your ball in the house."	
"Don't talk back to me."	
"Don't feel that way."	
"There's no reason to be angry."	
"Don't hit your brother when you're mad at him or feeling frustrated."	
"Don't run away from me in the parking lot."	
"Don't ignore me when I talk to you."	

BOUNDARIES AND LIMITS TIPS

In addition to incorporating more positive directions to guide behavior, here are some other pointers that will help your three-year-old be more responsive:

- Typically, you need to validate the feeling and then guide the behavior. Feeling felt is important to a child this age.
- Drop the "If you'll do . . . then I'll . . ." language. You're inviting a power struggle. Say, "First do . . . then you can . . . ." They are in control and doing estimable acts rather than deciding whether they feel like pleasing you.
- Help them identify the emotion that is driving the behavior. You can make guesses by saying, "I wonder if you're feeling . . . ." You can do this without addressing the unwelcome behavior. You're helping them feel felt while ignoring the tantrum.
- Once you know the emotion, offer an alternative. "When you start feeling jealous, come get me, and I will help you deal with that tough feeling."
- Use "Let's do . . ." language. Rather than "Go wash your hands," say, "Let's wash your hands." Three-year-olds like to connect and are more likely to comply with behaviors that they feel are communal.

DISCIPLINE

Throughout this chapter, I have offered a few tips for guiding the behavior (and soothing the temper) of your three-year-old. We have discussed the importance of connecting first, the value in parent self-control and reflection, and the importance of helping your child "feel felt" before redirecting. We have worked to get in the habit of joining with your child to troubleshoot solutions for unwelcome behaviors. I have also reminded you that your three-year-old responds best when you tell them *what to do* instead of always relying on prohibitions and scolding to shape behavior.

The final piece in three-year-old discipline, boundaries, and wellness activities is the intentional incorporation of praise. This involves identifying target behaviors ahead of time and working hard to catch your child in the act of meeting your expectations. Once you get in the habit of using more positive behavior guidance rather than prohibitions, noticing the target behaviors will become much easier.

FINDING AND PRAISING
TARGET BEHAVIOR

You may want to revisit the questions in the last chapter's Boundaries and Routines section. There, I asked you to consider your family's values and the type of community member you would like your child to become. Knowing these values and imagining this esteemed community member is a helpful exercise in identifying the behaviors you *want to see* in your child.

Here, I will list a few of the broad expectations that many parents have for their children and then give you the opportunity to make a plan to praise. You'll identify the target behaviors involved in that skill set or value set. Once you have these established, then you can watch closely and praise those behaviors.

Many families have a massive praise deficit. They rely solely on scolding or prohibitive direction and rarely guide behavior with positive direction and praise. It is a very easy mistake to make. When families with a praise deficit introduce praise and become intentional about watching for target behaviors, things begin to change—almost overnight. If you're one of those parents that feels like "nothing is working," it might be because you have a deficit that needs fixing.

List the target behavior that accompanies each of the following expectations. I've started you off.

Parental expectation	Target behaviors
Being well-mannered at the table	* Staying in the chair * Chewing with their mouth closed * Thanking the cook * Using their napkin
Sharing with siblings	
Being helpful during the morning and night routines	
Acting with respect toward adults	

Now consider a behavior set that you want for your child or a particular prohibition that you have been repeating over and over. For me, it's "No running in the house!" *What is yours?*

_____

_____

How might you break this value set, or even the prohibition that you are repeating frequently, into a few target behaviors you can praise?

1. _____

2. _____

3. _____

4. _____

5. _____

TURNING VALUES INTO PRAISE

Another way of thinking through these questions about praise and target behaviors is to bring to mind your family's treasured values and people. I asked you about these in the previous chapter (see page 122). Which value did you recall?

_____

When you recall a picture of someone meeting your expectations or exhibiting this value, what kinds of micro-behaviors do you notice?

_____

_____

One of our big family values is *kindness*. I bet you share that one, too. Now, let's put flesh on kindness. I mean: Let's really imagine the daily activities of a kind person. What kind of things do they do?

_____

_____

_____

Now you can begin to catch your child doing the behaviors you have listed. Get in there. Discipline is so much more than scolding and prohibitions; it is shaping behavior through praise, guidance, and respect!

INTERACTION TALLY

Behaviors we examine and record are more likely to change. I have personally experienced this with dozens of families in my office. Many parents bring troubling family dynamics into my office and are surprised to hear me wonder about their ratio of positive interactions to negative interactions. I want to know how often they *scold and prohibit* compared with how often they *praise or admire*. Many parents either don't know or make a guess that ends up being inaccurate.

When it comes to discipline, positive interactions are the most effective intervention. You should know with certainty how often you are engaging in each type of behavior.

Here I offer you the same simple exercise I offer in my office. Typically, I draw this on an index card and ask the parent to keep it near the family's hub (usually the kitchen). I simply want you to put a mark for every positive interaction you have with your child in the first column. Mark negative interactions in the other. Obviously, not all these things in the second column are inherently "bad," but for the sake of this exercise, we need to clearly determine what proportion of negative or positive experiences we are sharing with our children.

Positive interactions this week	Negative interactions this week
Positive directions	Scolding
Help	Prohibiting
Open conversation	Criticizing
Shared laughter	Sarcasm
Encouragement	Anger
Praise	

MARBLE FUN

They say token economies (using good behavior as currency in the home) doesn't work for kids—but who said anything about parents? Let's be clear: This exercise is for you.

I want you to go online or to your local craft store and buy 25 marbles. Also, you'll need two jars. Mark one jar with a minus sign and one jar with a plus sign. Put one marble in the "+" jar for starting this activity and keep the rest in a bag or drawer nearby.

Now, determine a reward for yourself for getting 25 positive interactions into the "+" jar. Write the reward here:

_____

Every time you have a positive interaction with your child, through either an act of praise and encouragement, laughing, sharing, or mutual care, I want you to drop a marble in the happy ("plus sign") jar. You will also put a marble in this jar every time you manage to direct your child's behavior in a way that is positive and clear, like "Please set the table" rather than "Why aren't you helpful? Stop sitting there!"

Anytime you engage in an act of criticism, sarcasm, prohibition, or scolding, I want you to take a marble out of the positive jar and put it in the negative ("minus sign") jar.

Note: The point of this exercise isn't shame. I am *not about shame*. It is about noticing how often you engage in one activity over the other. It is about noticing how hard it is to introduce new behavioral patterns into your family and make changes.

If you have some time or if you think it will be helpful, you may want to answer a few questions. They aren't necessary but may support your endeavor.

What are some of your favorite things about your child?

_____

_____

What are some treasured values that you can reinforce during this time?

_____

_____

What are the behavioral traps or verbal phrases you use that you would like to avoid?

_____

_____

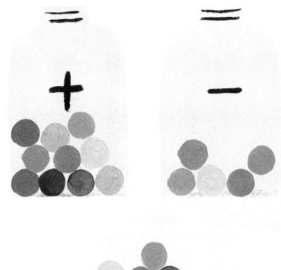

CHAPTER FIVE

4
YEAR-OLDS

Unless your child has a younger sibling running around, you're officially out of the toddler phase. A four-year-old is a tenacious and curious child. Their language is impressive, their motor skills are honed, and their problem-solving skills provide endless entertainment and pleasure. They are starting to transition into school environments, and the onus of cognitive growth and training is beginning to transfer to places outside the home. This is why four-year-old children are often called preschoolers.

Over the course of this book, our exercises and opportunities have gone from focusing on learning and wellness activities, with very little emphasis on discipline, to almost a complete focus on behavior guidance techniques and temper management.

All along, parent self-control, thoughtfulness, and connection have been our guideposts. This remains true in this chapter, but now the lines between wellness and learning, boundaries and discipline, become blurred. As your child has aged, these once (somewhat) disparate areas have become integrated, intertwined, and collaborative, each playing off and contributing to the other.

Over the next several years, this continued integration will be the goal. Moments of dis-integration, when their logic and boundaries stop working together or their self-care separates from their self-discipline, will be the moments that put our parenting skills to the test. Those are times when we have to offer our calming presence and wisdom.

FOUR-YEAR-OLD MILESTONES

Muscles

Your child has a robust repertoire of motor skills. They can balance on one foot, hop up and down, and pedal a tricycle. They can feed themselves, put their shoes on, brush their teeth, and get dressed. You may notice a hand preference solidifying as they color and draw. The shapes they draw should begin to resemble what the child has intended.

Language and Communication

Language and communication with a four-year-old continue to be a joy. They speak in full sentences and, when comfortable, can communicate well with adults. They use pronouns correctly and say most words intelligibly and clearly, even though they may have some regular articulation errors (unable to say "th" or "r" sounds). They can also follow multiple-part instructions (believe it or not, they can) and will recognize a few letters, numbers, and words. They can tell you what they like and do not like with ease. They also know the names of their friends.

Social and Emotional

One of the big developments for four-year-olds is just how sophisticated their play has become. They can happily engage in either solo (alone) or associative (together) play. They might coordinate their motor skills in fun ways for games of tag or chase on the playground, but it is the most fun to watch the way your four-year-old will coordinate peers for a game of make-believe. They can tell stories and play multiple parts, building fun narratives and interesting scenarios. Some kids get a lot of pleasure from creating art on their own and being alone, but when necessary they can play with other children and join in the games that others have imagined.

Intelligence

Four-year-olds' thinking and problem-solving skills are also becoming increasingly sophisticated. They enjoy learning new things and can work hard to remember fun facts and jokes. They can recognize a few colors, letters, numbers, and symbols and can write their name. Many children enjoy going to a preschool environment a few days a week to practice their wonderful new skills—skills that are growing every day.

WELLNESS

In chapter 2, I introduced the different elements of *temperament* (intensity of reaction, frustration tolerance, activity level, coping with change, and reactions to new people) and asked you to locate your child on the continuum of each element. I also asked you to mark a place where you feel that you might fall on each continuum.

Please take time now to redo those exercises (see page 75).

One of the biggest mistakes that parents with children this age make is failing to be optimally responsive to the unique temperament of their child during times of discipline and boundary-making. They also forget to attend to the unique ways each child interacts with the parent's own temperament. This is unfortunate because temperament recognition and parental attunement continue to be two of the great contributors to child health and well-being.

This section is meant to help you reconnect to your child's unique needs so that you can more intentionally structure your interactions and care during these formative years.

GOODNESS OF FIT

As you look back over the temperament exercises in chapter 2, you can see that there is no better or worse place on the continuum of each trait. Highly active learners more easily stave off obesity, while slow-to-warm children tend to be risk-averse and stay safe. Each trait provides strengths or challenges according to that trait's fit with different caregivers and different environments.

Goodness of fit refers to how compatible the demands and expectations of an environment are with a person's temperament, expectations, and preferences. For the purposes of this exercise, it refers to how well an *adult* can recognize and respond (or adapt) to a *child's* temperament. So, let's explore more about your temperament and compare it with your child's.

SIMILARITIES

What traits do you and your child have in common?

_____

_____

_____

Do these similarities help you get along?

Yes / No

Do any challenges come up because of these similarities?

Yes / No

Think about the challenges that you have overcome, how you overcame them, the ways you were supported, and the ways you wish your parents had noticed your inclinations or supported you differently.

What are the ways you can support your child, given your similarities?

_____

_____

_____

_____

_____

DIFFERENCES

What traits do you *not* have in common with your child?

_____

_____

Do these differences help you get along?

Yes / No

Do any challenges come up because of these differences?

Yes / No

Think about the ways and times that you wish your caregivers had been more patient or had challenged themselves to offer you support.

What are the ways you can support your child, given your differences?

_____

_____

_____

_____

_____

TEMPERAMENT-BASED PARENTING

As I noted previously, one of the most common mistakes that parents make is the way they fail to take temperament into account when disciplining (or teaching) their child.

Temperament-based parenting happens when caregivers:

1. Practice what they preach.
2. Model their own struggle, growth, and hard-earned tools.
3. Adjust their techniques to fit the child.

PRACTICE WHAT YOU PREACH

We need to respect our children and show them the values we want them to manifest. We do this through the way we interact with them and the way we interact with our peers—especially their other parent, their other caregivers, and your partner.

Consider the values and behaviors you would like to see from your child as you answer the following questions:

How would you characterize the tone and content of your interactions with the child's other parent or your partner?

_____

_____

_____

Are you regularly using the same language and tone with them and others that you would like to see from your child?

Yes / No

What are the similarities between the way your child treats their sibling(s), friends, or their other caregivers and the way that you speak to and interact with your child or with your partner?

_____

_____

_____

Many parents expect their children to say "Please" and "Thank you" as a sign of respect. Do you regularly use these expressions with your child?

Yes / No

How do you show your child respect?

_____

_____

Of the ways you expect your child to demonstrate respect for you and their elders, are you regularly modeling this in your interactions with them?

Yes / No

Do you look your child in the eye? Wait until they are finished to begin talking? Use a gentle and respectful tone with discussing tough stuff? In what ways could you improve?

_____

_____

_____

MODELING YOUR STRUGGLE AND YOUR TOOLS

Oftentimes, angry and/or anxious parents bring stressed and combustible kids in to see me. This is fine when the parent acknowledges the similarity and begins to work on themselves so that they can provide assistance to their children.

I occasionally have to remind parents: "Listen, you gave this child your brain—now help them drive it!" I am joking, of course, but in many ways it is true. You and your child likely have a few powerful struggles in common. Dig in, do the work yourself, and then share your revelations. The things that work for you are more likely to work for them!

When you consider your temperament and its many variations, what is one area of overlap you can remember struggling with or currently resent still having to deal with daily?

_____

_____

_____

Children typically have trouble paying attention and managing their anger, and they become easily scared, shy, or anxious. Have you ever struggled with any of these things? Which ones?

_____

_____

_____

What lessons or tools have you learned to manage those struggles? In what ways can you offer your wisdom and experience to your child?

_____

_____

_____

_____

_____

_____

ADJUSTING YOUR TECHNIQUES TO FIT THE CHILD

As you reconsider your child's temperament (and even the way it has taken shape over the past year), what traits are relevant to the way your child needs to be taught or disciplined?

_____

_____

Some children have personalities that make them easily flooded and thus unreceptive to instruction that is delivered in big tones and big body language. Does your child have a trait that seems to make teaching them particularly challenging for you?

_____

_____

How does this interact with your choices?

_____

_____

Considering your previous answers, are there better choices you could make? Do you have mannerisms that might make you difficult to receive?

_____

_____

Consult with a friend or colleague. Be creative and think outside your box. If your styles are regularly conflicting, then another set of eyes will be useful!

LEARNING

Hello, real world, here we come! More than ever, your child is ready to experience a kind of graduated, softer version of real-world learning. This has major implications: cause and effect, consequences, and rewards. As your child matures, it is possible (and necessary) to prioritize connection and care while still being firm, maintaining boundaries, and introducing *thoughtful* consequences.

Many parents have a go-to punishment: timeout, spanking, yelling, or taking away a privilege. You may be surprised to learn that the research is pretty clear that immediately defaulting to a standard punishment, regardless of the child's temperament or unwanted behavior, is actually counterproductive (not just ineffective). In this section, we will talk through the difference between default punishment and thoughtful consequences so that your child can continue their learning experience in a more real-world manner while still under your love and care.

CONSEQUENCES VERSUS PUNISHMENT

There's a rumor circling that parents should not use consequences because they are unkind and hurtful. This rumor started, I believe, as a reaction to the older, strictly behaviorist forms of discipline—in particular, spanking, yelling, and all forms of token economies, in which rewards are gained for good behavior and lost for bad behavior. These things aren't just ineffective, they are actually counter to most parent's goals and can produce *more* of the undesired behavior.

Still, the research regarding these very particular kinds of punishments and rewards doesn't mean that parents can't allow their children to experience naturally occurring consequences and dole out abundant (even profuse) praise. The trick, of course, is learning the difference between consequences and punishment so that you can avoid the things that are less effective and focus on the cause-and-effect sequences that produce results.

Punishments tend to be arbitrary and unrelated to the unwelcome behavior. A consequence, on the other hand, is more naturally related to the concerning behavior and attempts to replicate real-world cause and effect.

Here is an example of a typical punishment sequence:

Cause: The four-year-old intentionally throws their green beans on the floor, making a big mess while shouting, "I hate your cooking."

Punishment: The child's parent takes away the child's Legos while telling them, "We don't throw food."

A more appropriate *consequence* would have been to have the child pick the green beans off the floor and then wipe the floor with a wet cloth.

They won't clean up very well (you will have to help a bit), but that is okay. They will have experienced the natural consequence of their behavior, at least in some part. This would be best if the you also practiced some of the other tools we have been working on, like staying calm and interpreting the emotion. You could say, "You don't want to eat your green beans" while offering a more appropriate response.

When the child struggles with the consequence, perhaps because they can't go to the park if they won't don their shoes, then you'll be there to comfort them. Yes, you're a part of the limitation, but only nominally. In general, people don't travel outside the home without their shoes. That's the rule; your role is to help your child cope with that rule in appropriate ways, however unfair it seems to them.

Fill in the following table by finding an appropriate consequence for each behavior. It may help to think of the behavior in its simplest terms. (I've included a few examples to show you.) Doing this little reductive work can make identifying benevolent consequences second nature.

Behavior	Simplified	Consequence
Pulls all the books off the shelf	Making a mess	Has to clean up the mess
Screams and runs in house	Using outside energy instead of inside energy, which is unsafe	"You can lower your voice, or you can go outside. Maybe you really want to act and feel big. That is great, but you'll have to do it outside."
Refuses to take a nap	Becoming grumpier and less coordinated	Has to go to bed earlier or can't do valued afternoon activity without proper rest
Won't put on jacket before leaving for the park in winter	Dressing in unsafe attire	
Won't pick up their toys when asked		

Behavior	Simplified	Consequence
Draws on walls with markers		
Kicks the dog on purpose		

Occasionally, it is appropriate to offer consequences that include a choice. I try to do this whenever I can. In the example about screaming in the house, this consequence helps the child see that they can stop the behavior (lower their voice), or they can put the behavior in its correct context (go play outside). There is no judgment or anger from the parent, just a simple teaching moment that includes boundaries, limits, and consequences. I like this example because it also makes an important point: Consequences aren't implicitly negative or punitive. Rather, they are a part of life's natural order or a valued set of rules. Consequences should teach rather than punish.

CONSEQUENCE TROUBLESHOOTING

Is there an unwelcome behavior that your child regularly exhibits that you have had little luck in extinguishing? What is it?

_____

_____

What specific things have you done to address it?

_____

_____

When you look at the behavior and then think about it in its simplest terms, what is the natural consequence of a behavior like this?

_____

_____

What is an appropriate limit that will keep this consequence from occurring in the future?

_____

_____

Is this something you can implement at home, and then hopefully, support them as they come to terms with it?

Yes / No

If you can't implement a version of the behavior's natural consequence at home (say the behavior is eating Play-Doh and the natural consequence is becoming ill), you'll have to intervene. "Humans can't eat things that make us sick. I have to take your Play-Doh away if you can't stop eating it."

This is a very helpful exercise as it helps us consider the path the child is on while looking at the natural destination of that path. Be careful; you don't want to assume your child is prison-bound for biting the neighbor's dog. Rather, look at the more immediate cause-and-effect relationship they have entered and do what is most natural to prevent the feared outcome. In this case, "Because you can't help but hurt the dog, you won't be allowed to play with him when we go visit the neighbor." When the consequence can be felt, at least nominally (as in cleaning the floor after a green bean wreckage), let them experience it: "It is annoying that we always have to clean up our messes. I know, and I am sorry. Let's get started."

⚮ DISCIPLINE ⚮

In the first few chapters, I offered basic calming tools to practice. This is because parent self-control truly is the key to all effective discipline. When the parent knows their triggers and can stay calm and be intentional about their actions, everything is easier and more effective. We've learned that a calm parent is also a parent who can continue to connect during difficult moments with their children. This ability matters because establishing a connection to the child and maintaining that connection throughout tough moments is imperative to all successful discipline. For them to be receptive to our guidance, we need them to feel felt and seen, especially when we are being firm and establishing new boundaries that they dislike.

In this section, I offer one final calming technique. This one has an element of self-reflection and happens to be a client favorite . . . and a favorite of mine.

If you haven't reviewed chapter 4, I encourage you to do so now. Not only did we discuss the priority of connection in discipline, we also discussed using time-ins (versus timeouts), how to use positive directions rather than prohibitions, and how to involve children's burgeoning problem-solving skills to troubleshoot problem behaviors at home. All these things continue to be valuable tools when parenting four-year-olds.

After the new calming and self-reflection technique that follows, our book will come to a close: Whew! You made it! I encourage you to move on to the bonus discipline section that immediately follows. Rather than dive into the specifics of behavior troubleshooting and management in the four-year-old section, I wanted to create a bonus section that could be used as a guide for all ages and stages. Our sweet one-year-old parents, who might just now be starting the book, will hopefully feel more included in our tips and techniques by proceeding in this manner. Have fun, and good luck. Discipline at all ages can be a challenge but shouldn't be a burden. The thrust should be connection, care, and teaching, not punishment.

CALMING TECHNIQUE: NONJUDGMENTAL REFLECTION

Observe your "self" as though you were observing a painting. Pretend that you don't know the painting, the artist, or the inspiration. Observe without quality assessment or judgment. Just notice.

WHAT AM I FEELING?

- ☐ Angry
- ☐ Sad
- ☐ Content
- ☐ Happy
- ☐ Surprised
- ☐ Tired
- ☐ Impatient
- ☐ Satisfied
- ☐ Overwhelmed
- ☐ Jealous

- ☐ Frustrated
- ☐ Fascinated
- ☐ Joyful
- ☐ Grateful
- ☐ Incompetent
- ☐ Hurt
- ☐ Scared
- ☐ Silly
- ☐ _____

WHAT AM I THINKING?

- ☐ This again?
- ☐ What is wrong with them?
- ☐ Why can't I figure this out?
- ☐ Who is to blame? Is this my fault?
- ☐ Why won't this child learn?
- ☐ Positive parenting doesn't work.

- ☐ I am a terrible parent.
- ☐ I give up.
- ☐ This kid is rotten.
- ☐ I am losing control.
- ☐ _____

WHAT AM I DOING?

- ☐ Yelling
- ☐ Crying
- ☐ Smiling
- ☐ Dancing
- ☐ Fidgeting
- ☐ Arguing
- ☐ Ignoring
- ☐ Being sarcastic
- ☐ Being punitive
- ☐ Dissociating

- ☐ Trying to win
- ☐ Threatening
- ☐ Belittling
- ☐ Serving
- ☐ Loving
- ☐ Giving
- ☐ Laughing
- ☐ Calming down
- ☐ Becoming agitated
- ☐ _____

WHAT CAN I DO INSTEAD?

- ☐ Nothing, I am exactly as I should be.
- ☐ Get a sip of water.
- ☐ Step outside into the sun.
- ☐ Splash water on my face.
- ☐ Take a deep breath.
- ☐ Squat down to be on my child's level.

- ☐ Smile and relax my shoulders.
- ☐ Have a snack.
- ☐ Listen reflectively and empathetically.
- ☐ Focus on connection.
- ☐ Tell myself there is no winner or loser.
- ☐ _____

Do this three times a day for three days. Then describe your experience.

_____

_____

CHAPTER SIX

DISCIPLINE, DISCIPLINE, DISCIPLINE

In a great many ways, this whole book has been about discipline. Consequently, having a chapter specifically dedicated to discipline might feel redundant. I can assure you, however, that there are still a few specific variables, attitudes, tips, and tricks that we can discuss that will help guide your disciplinary interventions and make your parenting *even more* effective.

We have already covered several of the core parenting competencies that contribute to effective teaching and behavior management (also known as discipline):

* Staying calm (see page 28)
* Connecting first (see page 130)
* Identifying target behaviors (see page 149)
* Using directions more than prohibitions (see page 146)
* Increasing your attention to value-affirming behavior (see page 92)
* The differences between consequences and punishments (see page 167)
* Using time-ins (see page 144)
* Involving the child in problem solving (see page 141)

All these things contribute to an environment that prioritizes connection and reinforces the attitude that *teaching rather than punishment* is at the core of all discipline. Several of the things that we covered, like the HALT questions (see page 24) and the instructions about validating feelings (see page 117), were meant to specifically address tantrum intervention. There is a lot of overlap between tantrum intervention and disciplinary action, but the two kinds of events are different and may, at times, require nuanced care.

"Bad" Behavior and Tantrums

Throughout the book, I have maintained the position that all behavior is communication and therefore is never accurately described as "bad." However, there are consequential behaviors (damaging, hurtful, or potentially dangerous), and there are behaviors that we simply want to extinguish or hope to stop. Typically, these inconsequential behaviors are either annoying or not value-affirming. (You can review the exercise about determining values and value-affirming behavior on page 122.) For this reason, many parents call this behavior "bad." For simplicity, I will refer to these types of inconsequential behaviors when I use the word *bad*.

Unlike bad behavior, a *tantrum* is a neurological event that represents a dis-integration of the brain's higher functioning. During tantrums, the child might display several bad behaviors, but there is *also* a loss of rational thinking, tears, and agitation. During a tantrum, reason jumps ship and leaves the child with a boat full of big emotions and suffering. During tantrums, I encourage you to stay calm, consider the cause, empathize, and offer alternatives (see page 26). During tantrums, I suggest that you ignore the bad behavior but not the child. I encourage you to connect in a way that really tends to the child and shares your valuable resources for calm. You're asking why and trying to help, teach, and care in a specifically attentive way. However, this isn't necessarily effective when *disciplining garden-variety bad behavior*. During moments of discipline, we don't want to engage with the bad behavior even enough to ask why (at least not in the moment).

When you treat your child as though a tantrum is simply bad behavior to be disciplined and thus withdraw your attention totally until the experience has resolved, you're leaving your child alone at a time when your resources are necessary. But when you over-empathize during simple and less neurologically motivated "bad behavior," you fall into a trap of using logic, overexplaining, and giving the behavior too much attention. During a tantrum, your attention is an anchor in the storm. During moments of bad behavior, your attention on the behavior is an affirmation to continue.

I wanted to briefly bring up this overlap so that when I describe the appropriate way to respond to simple bad behavior, like hitting, biting, mess-making, refusing, and various forms of un-kindness, it is clear that I am *not talking about tantrums*. You should never ignore the child during a tantrum, and you should not over-empathize during bad behavior.

WHAT TO DO WHEN CHILDREN MISBEHAVE

When your child misbehaves (that is, acts in a way that is not value-affirming), first ask yourself the following questions:

1. How likely is this behavior to cause harm?
2. How likely is this behavior to persist?
3. How likely is it that this *inconsequential behavior* (teasing a sibling) will become a *consequential behavior* (fighting to hurt)?

If the likelihood for all these is low:

1. Ignore the behavior.
2. Find other appropriate behaviors to reinforce.

If the likelihood for *even one* of these is high:

1. Don't just stop the consequential behavior; *tell them what to do*. If you need help with this, review page 146.
2. Only if needed, respond briefly with empathy *to their reaction to the boundary*. Some boundaries are hard to understand for children because they don't see the impending harm. You do. Have a little sympathy for their lack of understanding.
3. Get them to do something appropriate and then reinforce the appropriate behavior. Focus on what the child is expected to do. Stay calm, pay attention, and stay especially connected to moments of target behavior.
4. Anticipate behavior based on past behavior. Listen, if you know your child loves jumping on furniture (a huge no-no at our house) and you are about to go to a party at a stranger's home, share a consequence couplet in the car: "If you jump on the furniture, you won't be asked back to visit" or "If you jump on the furniture, we will go home immediately."
5. Check yourself before you wreck yourself.

   * **Don't overexplain,** especially *in the moment*. Ignore the behavior. If you have to revisit it, do so carefully and later. Don't make the bad behavior a part of their story. Do the minimal explanation to avoid the trap of being critical, causing shame, and inadvertently encouraging a repeat occurrence.
   * **Don't use logic,** especially in the moment.
   * **Don't ask, "Why?"** Most of the time your child doesn't know, and you shouldn't care enough about the bad behavior to get an answer. Just let it go and find something you'd love to reinforce. Children are impulsive. When you ask why they engage in an impulse they can't help, they internalize it in ways that would make your heart sad.
   * **Don't use force** (see page 123). It doesn't work, and it is uncomfortable for everyone in your household.

WHAT TO DO WHEN CHILDREN ‿‿ BEHAVE WELL ‿‿

No matter your recent or frequent frustrations, your child often behaves well. Especially when things are difficult and problem behavior seems to be growing, we need to be watching and noticing on-target and value-affirming behavior. A few common target behaviors are:

* Making the bed
* Picking up toys
* Setting the table
* Sharing
* Being kind or generous to a sibling or friend
* Brushing their teeth
* Getting dressed
* Putting their shoes away

A random schedule of reinforcement has been shown to be the most effective. Casually watch, notice, and acknowledge the target behaviors frequently. It isn't necessary to acknowledge their "good" behavior every time, just often.

Tips for Discipline-Oriented Praise

1. **Be casual and plentiful.** There is no need to make a big show and stop everything you're doing. If you can be casual about your disciplinary praise, then you are more likely to keep it up. Make a *habit*, not a *production*, of praising target behaviors.

2. **A touch, wink, smile, and verbal affirmation** are the four best simple praise tactics.

3. **Be descriptive.** When we are praising to shape and teach (that is, disciplining), then we need to occasionally be quite descriptive and specific. Simply saying, "You're so great," isn't nearly as effective as saying, "I love the way you put your shoes away without asking." *You are praising behavior*, not making vague character assessments.

4. **Acknowledge the value that you see.** In addition to being specific, occasionally you should let them know *why* that behavior is great. For instance, "You're helping keep the house clean, which makes me feel loved. Thank you." or "Feeding the dog is such a sweet way to care for our animals. You're becoming so responsible." I try to always add a "Thank you."

DISCIPLINE TROUBLESHOOTING

Let's tie everything we have discussed about discipline thus far into a simple, clarifying opportunity. Hopefully, this exercise will help you think through a plethora of difficult situations as your child continues to age. The questions are simple but strategic, and with any luck, you'll soon be noticing that a little forethought goes a very long way when it comes to effective discipline.

What is one of your child's problem behaviors with which you are struggling or struggle with daily?

_____

_____

_____

_____

_____

When and in what setting(s) does this behavior typically occur?

_____

_____

Note: These are moments when you can be prepared for difficult behavior and when you can be on the lookout for target behavior. Preparing and predicting future incidents is wise, as it helps you help your child while also getting you in the right frame of mind for difficult scenarios.

Is this behavior consequential? Is it likely to become destructive or harmful?

Yes / No

If it is unlikely to become harmful to the child or someone else, you can (and probably should) ignore it.

What are some other more appropriate behaviors you could notice and praise in this setting?

_____

_____

After ignoring the bad behavior, how might you be able to redirect the child toward these more appropriate behaviors?

_____

_____

_____

_____

What are one or two consequence couplets for these good behaviors?

_____

_____

Note: When you are introducing positive consequences, it is best to use language like "When you do [positive behavior], then we can [positive consequence or privilege]" rather than "If you do [negative behavior], then I will [negative consequence]." It gives your child power and makes their actions more estimable.

What are one or two consequence couplets for the bad behaviors?

_____

_____

Note: You do not have to share these couplets with your child. Rather, they are good to for you to know so you can be firm, decisive, and consistent. Consider again the difference between punishments and consequences (see page 167).

What are one or two consequence couplets for the value-affirming behaviors?

_____

_____

Note: These are great to share in the "When you do . . . then we can . . . ." format.

If you expect a response from the child (for example, "But he had it coming!"), how might you briefly respond with empathy before quickly redirecting the behavior toward something you can praise?

_____

_____

_____

CONCLUSION

If I had to summarize the entire book in two lines, it would go something like this:

> Stay in the relationship by offering your loving attention, tender care, and appropriate responses.
>
> Be affirming, don't be afraid to apologize when you mess up, and make sure that you're modeling the values that you hope to see in your child.

As a parent or a primary caregiver, you are *the* powerhouse of world-changing action, kindness, and love. With your steadied influence and well-intentioned care, you can and *will* make the difference in your child's life (and character) that will affect your community, your city, your country, and the world.

You aren't just raising a child, you are raising one of this world's future leaders—one of our future thinkers and innovators, creators, presidents, executives, teachers, or servants. Together with your peers—the women and men at the soccer fields and PTA meetings—you are raising a kid in the generation that needs to know what it means to value connection over victory, patience over intolerance, forgiveness over injury, and hope over despair. *They learn these values and become these types of leaders in your home.* Continue the good work and change the future.

RESOURCES

3 in 30 Takeaways for Moms (https://3in30podcast.com) is my favorite parenting podcast, available wherever podcasts are served.

Center on the Developing Child at Harvard University (developingchild.harvard.edu) is another great website with helpful publications.

Everything Tina Payne Bryson writes with Dan Seigel is perfect.

Zero to Three (zerotothree.org) is a great website.

REFERENCES

Center on the Developing Child at Harvard University. "Brain Architecture." Accessed March 19, 2015. https://developingchild.harvard.edu/science/key-concepts/brain-architecture.

Center on the Developing Child at Harvard University. "The Foundations for Lifelong Health are Are Built in Early Childhood." Accessed February 28, 2020. https://developingchild.harvard.edu /resources/the-foundations-of-lifelong-health-are-built-in-early-childhood.

Chesley, Noelle. "Information and Communication Technology Use, Work Intensification, and Employee Strain and Distress." *Work, Employment, Society* 28, no. 4 (August 2014): 598–610.

Council on Communications and Media. "Media Use by Children Younger Than 2 Years." *Pediatrics* 128, no. 5 (November 2011): 1040–45.

Jago, Russell, Emmanuel Stamatakis, Augusta Gama, Isabel Mourão Carvalhal, Helena Nogueira, Vítor Rosado, and Cristina Padez. "Parent and Child Screen-Viewing Time and Home Media Environment." *American Journal of Preventative Medicine* 43, no. 2. (2012): 150–58.

Kemp, Christine J., Erica Lunkenheimer, Erin C. Albrecht, and Deborah Chen. "Can We Fix This? Parent-Child Repair Processes and Preschoolers' Regulatory Skills." *Family Relations* 65, no. 4 (October 2010): 576–90.

Kirkorian, Heather L., Tiffany A. Pempek, Lauren A. Murphy, Marie E. Schmidt, and Daniel R. Anderson. "The Impact of Background Television on Parent-Child Interaction." *Child Development* 80, no. 5 (2009): 1350–59.

Radesky, Jenny, Alison L. Miller, Katherine L. Rosenblum, Danielle Appugliese, Niko Kaciroti, and Julie C. Lumeng. "Maternal Mobile Device Use during a Structured Parent-Child Interaction Task." *Academic Pediatrics* 15, no. 2 (2015): 238–44.

Radesky, Jenny S., Caroline J. Kistin, Barry Zuckerman, Katie Nitzberg, Jamie Gross, Margot Kaplan-Sanoff, Marilyn Augustyn, and Michael Silverstein. "Patterns of Mobile Device Use by Caregivers and Children during Meals in Fast Food Restaurants." *Pediatrics* 133, no. 4. (2014): e843–e849.

Reid Chassiakos, Yolanda (Linda), Jenny Radesky, Dimitri Christakis, Megan A. Moreno, Corinn Cross, and the Council on Communications and Media. "Children and Adolescents and Digital Media." *Pediatrics* 138, no. 5 (2016): e20162593.

Schmidt, Marie Evans, Tiffany A. Pempek, Heather L. Kirkorian, Anne Frankenfield Lund, and Daniel R. Anderson. "The Impact of Background Television on the Toy Play Behavior of Very Young Children." *Child Development* 79, no. 4 (2008): 1137–51.

Siegel, Daniel, and Tina Payne Bryson. *No-Drama Discipline: The Whole-Brain Way to Calm the Chaos and Nurture Your Child's Developing Mind*. New York: Bantam Books, 2016.

Tsabary, Shefali. *The Conscious Parent: Transforming Ourselves, Empowering Our Children*. New York: Namaste Publishing, 2010.

Zero to Three. "School Readiness: Foundations in Language, Literacy, Thinking, and Social-Emotional Skills." Accessed February 28, 2020. https://www.zerotothree.org/resources /195-school-readiness-foundations-in-language-literacy-thinking-and-social-emotional -skills#downloads.

INDEX

H

HALT acronym, 24–25

Hygiene, 11, 89

I

Imagination, 129

Intelligence, 6

    12-month-olds, 35

    18-month-olds, 71

    two-year-olds, 103

    three-year-olds, 129

    four-year-olds, 158

Interactions

    debriefing, 131–133

    tallying, 152–154

L

Language and communication skills, 6, 13

    12-month-olds, 34

    18-month-olds, 70

    two-year-olds, 102

    three-year-olds, 128, 138–140

    four-year-olds, 158

Learning, 12–15

    12-month-olds, 47–53

    18-month-olds, 81–87

    two-year-olds, 107–112

    three-year-olds, 137–143

    four-year-olds, 167–171

Limits, setting, 121–122

Logic, 141

M

Mealtimes, 20–21

Milestones, 6–7

    12-month-olds, 33–35

    18-month-olds, 69–71

    two-year-olds, 101–103

    three-year-olds, 127–129

    four-year-olds, 157–159

Misbehavior, 179–180

Muscle development, 6

N

Naps, 11–12

Natural consequences, 94–95, 167–171

Nature vs. nurture, 3–4

Nightmares, 18

Night terrors, 18

Nonverbal communication skills, 6

Nurturance, 73–74

Nutrition. *See* Diet and nutrition

O

Oral motor skills, 6

ACKNOWLEDGMENTS

To the adults in my practice who have trusted me to listen and to mourn the simple ways you could have been loved as a child but weren't. This book is your book. I wrote it for your mother and your father—good men and women who meant to love you but didn't know how, who wanted to connect but didn't have the resources. Even now, I write this with tears on my cheeks and a deep longing in my chest. Like you, I wish I could go back in time and shepherd them in the simple ways of connection and love. I wish I could have reminded them, one morning right before you were born, to hold you when you cried, to apologize when you hurt, to recognize your character, your preferences, and your power. At the very least, may our conversations turn into fruit that future generations can eat and be fed, that they may acquire the simple skills of loving wonderful children like you and of loving them *well*.

ABOUT THE AUTHOR

 **KATIE PENRY** is a clinical psychologist, practicing on the Gulf Coast of Alabama. She received her doctorate from Wheaton College outside Chicago. Her website, *drkatiepenry.com*, serves parents internationally as a resource for parent support and research-driven wisdom. She has postdoctoral training in psychoanalysis and considers psychoanalysis to be her driving theoretical orientation. She has a son and a daughter. She's done residencies with many different populations in highly esteemed facilities. But her favorite job has been the daily, encouraging work she does in her own private practice.

ABOUT THE ILLUSTRATOR

 **PENELOPE DULLAGHAN** is an award-winning illustrator whose work includes illustrations for ad campaigns, book publishers, magazines, newspapers, products, videos, and most recently, children. Penny works from her home studio in Indianapolis, Indiana. There, she also homeschools her daughter, hikes and plays by the river behind her house, and tends to her front-yard vegetable garden.

CPSIA information can be obtained
at www.ICGtesting.com
Printed in the USA
LVHW070834180720
661055LV00020B/2523